Best Wishes
Ralph J. Hall

Thank You for
your friendship
that has blessed
my life

The Main
Trail

The Main Trail

by Ralph J. Hall

edited by Vic Jameson

The Naylor Company
Book Publishers of the Southwest
San Antonio, Texas

Foreword

A PROMINENT RADIO PREACHER of New York City said that he did not know of any preacher in the country who was reaching people for Christ and drawing them to be committed followers of Christ. He did not know Ralph Hall. From the time Ralph made his decision in a little schoolhouse in Texas to be a minister, he has never wavered from that commitment.

In his own boyhood on a ranch he knew how much a family could long for and pray for a minister to come and share the message of Christ with them. When an ordained Sunday School missionary did come, he brought that message and he also brought a call from the Holy Spirit for Ralph.

Ralph always had a humility, a sincerity and a spiritual depth in his life which reached deep into the lives of other people in personal contact. He loved people and was at once concerned for their physical and spiritual needs. He had a sense of compassion and people felt it. With that he poured his own soul into his preaching. Often he told the story of what God had done for him and then proceeded to tell his hearers what God could do for them. Thousands responded by pledging themselves to follow Christ, to be active for Him and to give of what they had — beef or cash — to share the good news about Him.

Little snatches of the spiritual power of this ministry drifted out to the national church. The church called upon him to go from coast to coast — to local churches, presbyteries, special conferences, church colleges and seminaries and to the General Assembly — and tell the story. Hundreds of people came from all over the country in travelling seminars to see and hear what was being done where it happened. The power of this spiritual life has touched people everywhere. It has led boys to decide to enter the ministry and adults to give generously to support the mission work of the church.

It has been my privilege to travel and camp out with Ralph alone and at camp meetings as we sought to visit lonely missionaries and lonely ranch people, and share the Gospel with them.

Needless to say, Ralph Hall has added much to the spiritual depth and breadth of my life. I could wish this for everyone.

There is much more to tell but let me invite you to open the pages of the story of this life and catch at least a portion of the spiritual depth which some of us have found who have known him intimately and have worked with him in sharing the good news of the Gospel of Christ.

Come and follow the trail.

J. Earl Jackman

Preface

ONE REGRET ABOUT PUBLISHING THIS is that it is impossible for me to begin to mention the names of all the great hosts of people and dear friends who have blessed and enriched my life with their love and friendship. If I tried to mention all their names I would be sure to leave out some who have made the greatest contributions.

This story has been written almost entirely from memory. As I approach my eightieth birthday I find my mind and memory are not what they were in years gone by. Until the time of my retirement I had a great many records of the years of service. When we moved into Plaza del Monte, we had only one small room for the two of us. Because we had no storage space, thinking the old records would be of little interest to anyone, and having no plan of writing a story of my life, we used them and made a good bonfire!

Had my ministry been spent in small parishes, names, places and dates would have been easy to remember. But my ministry has been across the nation. My particular parish has been across the great western cattle range country of several states. Therefore, this is no continuing story but a collection of memories from across the years. I have not tried to tell it in a strict chronological way, but just as the memories seem to fit together from those blessed years along the "Main Trail."

To all the dear friends who may read these stories, I send my greeting, gratitude and love.

Ralph J. Hall

Contents

List of Illustrations

Picture section between page xiv and 1.

Introduction

THIS IS RALPH HALL'S STORY. Others have tried to tell it, but with only limited success.

The simple truth is that none could match the words of the man who lived it.

No attempt has been made in the editing to embellish or stylize those plain and honest words. The only effort has been to let the remarkable man who is Ralph Hall come through in the limited capabilities of the printed page.

Vic Jameson

Old schoolhouse meeting, Lindreth, N.M.

Evening prayers at young people's conference

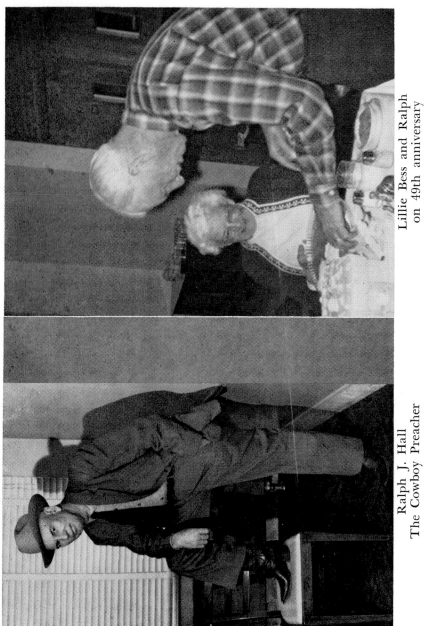

Ralph J. Hall
The Cowboy Preacher

Lillie Bess and Ralph
on 49th anniversary

Ralph and Roger

First traveling seminar

Ralph preaching at Reserve

Mealtime at a camp meeting

Ralph, Philadelphia Academy of Music

Chuck line at a camp meeting

Everett King presents D.D. degree to Ralph

Ralph at Nogal Mesa

The Beginning of the Dream

THE EARLIEST MEMORY I cherish is of my boyhood days at our home in the ranch country of West
Texas. We were a large family of five boys and five
girls. We were a busy family, but no matter how great the
pressure, I can never remember a time when Dad was too
busy to wait until each member of the family was at the
table. Then he would offer a short prayer of thanksgiving.

We got along pretty well through the week, but when
Sunday rolled around and there was no place to go for
worship services, a great blanket of loneliness seemed to
settle down over us. But in the afternoon we would gather
in the large living room, and with my sister playing the old
reed organ, we would sing Gospel hymns, have family Bible
readings, and memorize Scripture verses.

In the evening we always had family worship. Dad would
take the large family Bible and read to us. He did not preach
at us but often just talked to us about what he read.

Never will I forget his prayers there with his family.
I can remember many things he prayed for, but seemingly
to me, the thing he always prayed for most earnestly was for
the coming of a minister or missionary to our home and
community.

1

I remember one very special occasion when that prayer was answered: A Sunday School missionary came. I was standing just behind mother as she answered the door and a man standing there said, "I am Mr. Hardin, a minister, a Sunday School missionary. I have heard of you people and have come to see you." What a welcome my mother gave him.

I didn't wait any longer but rushed to the barn to tell Dad and my brothers there was a preacher at the house. Dad hardly took time to greet him before he asked how long our guest could stay and if we could have a preaching service. The minister replied he planned to stay over Sunday, so on Saturday we spread the news to all our neighbors and friends, telling them we had a minister at the house and were going to have dinner on the grounds of the schoolhouse Sunday and preaching all day.

Somehow and in some way, that Sunday was very special for me. I was so impressed by the large crowd that came. Whichever way I looked, I could see people coming in wagons, on horseback, in buggies. They crowded into that little schoolroom until it seemed to me they were going to push the walls out.

We had no organ nor other musical instrument, and not enough songbooks to go around. The minister would read one verse of a hymn and all would sing. Since then I have heard great choirs, but they never sounded as wonderful as that group singing together in that little schoolhouse that Sunday morning. There was a spirit of awe and reverence about it all that I have never forgotten.

I remember sitting beside that Christian, pioneer mother of mine as the minister stood up and began his sermon. I glanced up into her face and for one of the few times in my life I saw tears rolling down her cheeks. I wondered why. I knew this was what she wanted more than anything in the whole world. I know now that they were tears of joy, at having her family, her neighbors and friends sitting there

2

under the sound of the Gospel being preached, worshipping together.

I think it was at that moment that a beautiful dream came into my heart, a dream that would not go away. In the days following this preacher's visit, as I went about my work on the range, in my boyish fancy I pictured myself as a minister going out across the range country telling the Gospel story. I felt that if someday I could find a home, a community as lonely and isolated as ours was, and if I could take something of the same joy and comfort into their hearts as Mr. Hardin brought to us, that life would indeed be full and rich, and that I would ask nothing more. The dream was with me day and night, never to go away.

As I grew older, seemingly insurmountable obstacles began to rise on the horizon and sometimes the road ahead seemed entirely blocked. The greatest drawback was that it looked like I would never be able to get an education. The chief reason was trouble with my eyes. They would not focus when I read and soon serious pain would come, but I was so self-conscious and shy I would not mention it to anyone. Mostly because of this I never went through a full term of school in my life; three or four months at a time was as long as I ever attended. I doubt if at any time of my life I could have passed a fifth-grade examination. I faked and stumbled along though, and soon I was a big, awkward, almost grown man with maybe a fifth-grade education. The beautiful dream was beginning to fade.

By this time a small church had been opened a few miles away. There were two preaching services each Sunday and always a prayer meeting each Wednesday evening. We usually attended as a family, but one Wednesday I attended alone. At the close of the service Mr. Powers, our minister, announced that he could not be present the next Wednesday evening and that someone else would have to lead the service. Then he looked around the group and said, "Ralph, will you lead the service?" I almost passed out. At the close of the service I rushed up to him to protest. He just would not listen and only said, "You'll do fine."

As I rode home through the darkness, I kept saying to myself, "I just can't do it." Then a bright thought came to me and I said, "Dad will do it for me." At breakfast the next morning I anounced very boldly that Dad was to lead the prayer meeting the next Wednesday evening. Dad looked at me with a twinkle in his eyes and said, "That's not the way I heard it."

Through the next week I thought of everything I had ever eaten that made me sick, of how I might have an accident. I even thought of saddling a horse and riding West, never to return. I could not find a way out and consoled myself by thinking I would never be asked to do it again. I knew I would make such a failure that no one would ever ask me again to say anything in public.

I had never done or said anything in public but once in my life, and that almost caused a riot. In the schoolroom and in class one day the teacher asked how a hen scratched for her food. I thought I was supposed to say that she scratched twice with her left foot and once with her right. I got up and stepped out in front of the class and proceeded to demonstrate, scratching twice with my left foot and once with my right. I never lived that down.

Finally, that dreaded Wednesday evening came. I had hoped and prayed for a bad storm but it did me no good. I don't think I ever saw so many people at prayer meeting. I had worked hard on what I planned to say and had practiced saying it to the cows, the chickens, and all the range stock. It certainly had not made any impression on them. I stepped up in the pulpit, knees knocking until I could hardly stand, hands shaking until I could hardly hold the Bible, and voice trembling until I could hardly speak. Perspiration rolled down my face. I was afraid I would forget what I wanted to say. I felt like the whole building would fall in on me. But after about two minutes something very

4

wonderful happened; I was not scared anymore. My voice was coming out strong, steady and clear. My knees were not knocking and the Bible did not shake anymore. I was remembering what I had planned to say and no one was laughing at me. Everyone seemed to be listening. I discovered it was wonderful to be up there speaking. Somehow it did not seem strange; I did not feel out of place; it just seemed right.

At the close of the service people came up to say kind and gracious things, that I did fine and that what I said was helpful. One lady said, "It just seemed so right for you to be standing up there preaching." Yes, she said "preaching." During the week before I had almost hated Mr. Powers for putting me in that position. Now, many years of preaching later, I am looking forward to hunting him up when I reach that Shore and saying a hearty "thank you" to him for giving me that privilege.

As I rode home that night I had a wonderful feeling. That beautiful dream of the small boy came alive, more real and precious than ever. But how could it ever come true, even if my eyes would permit me to study? How could I, an almost grown man, ever go back to school to take up fifth or sixth grade with small neighbor children?

At Brownwood, Texas, a hundred miles away, there was a small Presbyterian college, Daniel Baker. I decided I would go there and talk with the president and others. Maybe I could sit in on some classes or something. When I talked with the president, I told him of my dream and burning heart to be a lay missionary. I explained to him about my eyes. He knew my father and was very sympathetic and understanding. First he made an appointment for me with a fine eye doctor, an elder in the local church. The doctor examined my eyes carefully, gave me some eye drops, fitted me with glasses, and told me to try reading and studying some, but not for too long at a time.

I went back and talked with the dean of the college, again telling of my life and dreams. He said, "You go talk

5

with Miss Austin. I'll ask her to take you under her wing." Miss Austin, a gracious and kind lady made arrangements for me to sit in on some classes, and gave me a full hour of her time every day, mainly studying grammar. For a few weeks I seemed to be getting along fine and was very hopeful. Then, again my eyes flared up.

On a Sunday morning after church I met the eye doctor in the vestibule. He edged me over into a corner, pulled off my glasses, lifted my eyelids and looked at my eyes. He said, "Come to the office tomorrow afternoon." The memory of what happened in the doctor's office is hazy in my mind now. I know he put me on a table and worked on my eyes for a long time. Then he put heavy bandages on them and said, "Leave these on for five days." His secretary drove me home. After five days he took off the bandages, once more giving my eyes a close examination. Then he sat down and talked with me very kindly. He said, "Ralph, it is no use for you to try and study more now."

He told me that the Lord could use good laymen as well as ministers. "I think you had better go back home. Don't try to read but very little. Do something else. Maybe sometime you can use your eyes without too much difficulty, but not now. You might lose your sight. I am sorry, but you must not go to school now."

It was a terrible blow. I didn't want to go home. Somehow I had never been able to tell any of the family of my dream to be a missionary, and I couldn't bear to tell them now that the dream was so broken. My oldest sister had just married and she and her husband had moved to Barstow, Texas, out on the Pecos River. So I went to see them. They said, "Stay here and work for us for a while." The days for me then were very dark and gloomy. It seemed I had reached a dead end.

One day Sister told me about a cousin of ours who lived at Lovington, New Mexico. The Reverend Louis Cunningham was pastor of the little church there and also chairman of the Home Missions Committee for El Paso Presbytery.

Sister said he was working himself to death. At that time two great sections of the country were opening up for homesteaders and people were flocking from Texas, Oklahoma and other places. He was trying so hard to provide a ministry for them and desperately needed help. I began to wonder if maybe I might help him as a lay missionary.

Without telling anyone I wrote him a long letter telling him of my desire and dream, and asking him if he thought there might be a place where I could serve in the Presbyterian church. Once more the dream came alive — if I could maybe work as his helper, that would be something.

But I made the mistake of sending the letter to Loving instead of Lovington, New Mexico, and it was some two months reaching Louis Cunningham. Not knowing this I watched the mail very closely. I had asked him to answer soon. As the days passed by, and no letter came, I felt very badly to think that he did not care even to answer my letter. More dark days; the dream once more began to fade, but still would not go away.

A Time of Great Decision

I T WAS ABOUT THIS TIME that I learned the presiding elder of the Methodist church was to be preaching for a week in Pecos about eight miles away, and I decided to ride over and hear him. As I rode into town the church bell was ringing, and somehow it had a special meaning for me that night. Before he began preaching, the presiding elder said he hoped several things would be accomplished: One of them was that he would find someone willing to go into a new field in New Mexico. Large areas were being opened for homestead entry, and many fine people were establishing homes. He said there was a desperate need for someone in the name of the church to visit them in their loneliness, organize Sunday Schools and conduct services of worship. He asked if anyone knew of someone who could and would do this type of work and would be willing to go to Black Tower Circuit on a temporary basis. He hoped someone would volunteer, and I felt as if he were looking right at me.

For five days I stayed away from Pecos. Should I offer myself for the Black Tower Circuit? Could I do it? Would I be acceptable?

Saturday night came, next to the last of the services in

Pecos, and I could not stay away. I thought maybe someone had volunteered, but once more he made his plea for someone to go to the Black Tower Circuit. He said he was sorry no one had offered to go. At the close of the service I spoke to the minister at the door, and said I would like to know a little more about the mission field in New Mexico. He pictured to me the field and its needs, and I told him the story of my life, of my dreams and desires, my lack of education. I told him also that I had hoped to work in the Presbyterian church. He said, "Why don't you go up there and try it out? If the way ever opens for you to work in the Presbyterian church, we'll give you our blessing and say to you, 'Go.' " I said I would let him know the next day.

As we shook hands to say good night, he said, "I have a deep conviction that you're the man for Black Tower Circuit. I will save tomorrow afternoon so we can talk."

I rode out in the desert for the rest of that long night. Out there alone under the stars, I had to make my decision. Who was I, to presume that I could organize Sunday Schools and conduct services of worship? It was a night of real soul-searching in prayer and meditation. As the first streaks of dawn appeared in the east, I got down on my knees and made a complete surrender of my life to Almighty God, saying to Him, "Here I am, the most unfitted, unprepared, unworthy person in all Your Kingdom for the field of service that is calling to me. Here is my life, just as it is. I will go to Black Tower Circuit if You want me and can use me. Only by Your grace, strength and guidance can I do anything. I will go from here on, day by day, as the way opens. Please, dear God, let my dreams come true."

I went to my sister and her husband, and to Dr. Downing, the pastor of the Presbyterian Church in the little town of Barstow, and told them of my dreams and hopes, and of the offer to go to Black Tower Circuit. They all agreed I should go, and gave me their blessings. I went to confer with the presiding elder, who seemed very pleased with my decision. He told me I should get a team and buggy and meet him at the quarterly conference in Elida, New Mexico, about 350 miles away, in ten days. There we would meet with other ministers and representatives from the Black Tower Circuit and we would all talk and pray about it together.

The next big job was to secure a team and buggy and get on the road. I went to a fellow who was closing out his livery stable and told him what I wanted to do and what I needed.

"I'll have an outfit for you ready to go," he said. "I know about what you'll need. You just come on down in the morning and I'll have something for you."

Clyde Black, a good pal of mine, decided he would go with me as far as Carlsbad and help me get started. When we went down the next morning, the livery man said, "This is your buggy and here is the harness. The horses are out in the round corral. Get them and get out of town." One of the horses was one I had ridden a few times, called Geronimo. He was a real buckskin, built like a greyhound, with about a four-inch mustache, and always showed a lot of white in his eyes. The other was a little coal-black wild stallion. The two of them would weigh about twelve hundred pounds.

They were so small, and the singletrees on the double buggy so high that we could not keep them in the harness. They just turned around and looked at us and ran backwards. Finally, the little stallion got down and refused to get up. We poured a little kerosene around him and set it afire. It had to get pretty hot before he got the message. A Spanish fellow came along during the performance and said, "Ah, ha, he no quiere to go, huh!" So we called the horse "No Carrie," and he lived up to the name.

Finally two fellows on horseback snubbed our team to their saddle horns and led us out of town. We tied their tails together with bailing wire to keep them from turning around to gaze at us, and we were off in a long lope.

We camped that first night along the Pea Vine Railroad

10

that ran from Pecos to Carlsbad. There was a train about once a week on that line, and we had chosen the wrong day.

We took along a bushel of oats and canvas nose bags to feed the horses some grain, but we might as well have fed them rocks. They had never had a bite of grain in their lives. They reared and fought those nose bags. We had long stake ropes so we staked them to fence posts along the railroad, the only place available. About 2:00 A.M. a train came puffing and whistling down the tracks; the horses had never seen a train before, so of course they took off. I woke up in time to hear the train and to see the fire fly from the fence when the ponies hit it. No Carrie pulled up his post and lit out. Geronimo was still there the next morning, but on the other side of the fence.

We made it to Carlsbad just after dark, and thought we would put the ponies in a wagonyard for the night so we could feed them hay since they would not eat grain. We came to a streetlight before reaching the wagonyard. They had never seen a streetlight before, and when they saw their shadows as we drove under the light, they took to the brush. We had to circle around to get in at the back of the yard.

It was not the most promising start for my new career — but at least I was on the way.

The next morning Clyde turned back and I went on alone. It was a long, hard drive. Along the way many questions kept coming into my mind. Was I being foolish? Who was I to think I could organize Sunday Schools, preach a sermon and carry on the work on a field like the one that had been pictured to me? Should I turn around and go back? Then I would recall that prayer out there on the desert, in which I had made my vow to Almighty God. No, I could not turn about. I must go on.

In Elida I met the presiding elder and his committee including representatives from the Black Tower Circuit. To me they were an awesome looking group, but they were wonderful. I had a separate conference with the group from

11

the field I was to serve, and always I will cherish the memory of this group of people. I will remember one couple especially. "We have a son not much older than you are who is a minister in a little field down in Texas," they said. "You come on, and in our hearts you will sort of take his place. We will welcome you and stand back of you."

The committee voted to ask me to go and they had a sort of dedication service and sent me out. I told them again that if the way opened I wanted to work in the Presbyterian church and they all said, "We understand and will give you our blessings."

The next day I drove on with great anticipation of the days ahead. At Grady I found a little store and post office. The storekeeper's family had an extra room and took me in. They told me that the first service was to be Sunday in a little schoolhouse. I worked hard on my first sermon and was as nervous as a fellow ever gets when on Sunday morning I stood up to preach. The schoolhouse jam-packed to hear the new preacher boy, and the people were very gracious and told me how helpful the sermon was. I am sure it was a poor effort, but it made me feel so wonderful to have them say nice, appreciative things.

That first Sunday I preached three times. I only had the one sermon and of course, I repeated it at each place. The evening service was about ten miles from where I preached in the morning. Just as we began the service, to my great surprise, in walked about fifteen people who had attended the morning service. I tried to holler in different places, but I felt sorry for those folks who had traveled all those miles and had to hear the same talk again. Every place I went the people received me most cordially. How I did enjoy the time I spent there. Every day was rich and full.

After five weeks a letter came from Louis Cunningham. He had just received my letter, and said of course there was a place for me in the Presbyterian church and for me to come right on. There was a field waiting for me at Seminole, just across across the line in Texas, where I could make my headquarters and work out across the range country. I was very sorry to leave those good people who had been so gracious to me; but when I talked with them about the letter, they said I should go. Reluctantly I loaded the buggy and headed for Lovington.

I just traveled across the country, following cattle trails as there were no roads. I had already discovered that I did not need that team and buggy, but a saddle horse, and the trip toward Lovington convinced me. I got down in that scrub brush country with deep sand, and it was mean going with a buggy at best. Although I had driven Geronimo and No Carrie several hundred miles, I still had to keep their tails tied together to keep them in harness. One thing that was a great nuisance was the many gates I had to pass through. At each gate I had to drive up to the fence, get out and tie them to a post, open the gate, get back in the buggy, turn around and drive through the gate, turn back to the fence, tie them to the post, go back and shut the gate, then get back in and turn around to head down the road.

These ponies were constantly watching for a chance to take off without me and they made it more than once.

On this trip I thought I would teach the ponies to stand while I closed the gate. I tied a stout rope to the lines and wrapped the rope around the gate post. I wanted to see them really set back on their heels. They could be in a dead run within a few feet from a standing start, and I was already anticipating their surprise when they hit the end of the slack in the rope. But they had too much momentum and what happened was that the leather lines broke, and away they went at full speed. The suitcase, bedroll and everything else that was loose went ten feet into the air while they galloped over a hill and out of sight. All I could see was a big cloud of dust in the air. I picked up my scattered belongings, sat down on the bedroll, and wondered how far they had made it by this time. Soon I saw two cowboys coming, each of them with a horse snubbed to his saddle horn. The buggy was still right side up. As they rode up, one of them said, "This outfit belong to you?" I said, "It sure does," and soon I was packed and on my way again.

When I got within twenty miles of Lovington, old No Carrie learned a new trick. He would be trotting along and all of a sudden he would go down on his knees and roll over. I thought at first he was sick and that maybe he would die. As soon as I would get him loose from the buggy, though, he would get up and begin to graze. I would put him back in the harness and start on, and within a mile there would be a repeat performance. Pretty soon he would not get up at all. I was near a homestead place, so I asked the fellow if I could leave No Carrie and the buggy there, borrow a saddle and go on. The man graciously agreed, so I put a saddle on Geronimo and rode the rest of the way to Lovington. I should have given up on the buggy, or on old No Carrie, right then; but it turned out I had one more lesson coming.

The Cunninghams were living in a homestead and didn't have much room, but they had an old covered wagon down by the barn and gave it to me for living quarters. I had a cot to sleep on, and it was wonderful.

I had a lot of fun the first night, after I discovered that there was an old setting hen on her nest under the cot. I would reach down and grab her, and she would squall. Louis would come charging out of the house barefoot and in his nightshirt, carrying his rifle and hollering at the dog to "sic em." He thought sure that some varmint had one of his chickens. It was a varmint all right, but not the kind he thought.

Louis sent me over to Knowles to preach for him on Sunday. Monday he told me to pack up and drive the fifty miles to Seminole and look up a family by the name of Brennand, who would help me get settled.

I got into Seminole late in the afternoon and drove up to the watering trough on the public square to water my team — my first glimpse of my new home and field of

14

service. A lot of cowboys were sitting around on the green grass under the shade trees on the courthouse square. As I drove up to the water trough, that ornery No Carrie put his head down under the neck yoke to drink instead of putting it over, as he should have. I knew when he raised up with the yoke over his head there would be a show, and I didn't want to make a scene there before those cowboys. I wanted to make a good impression on my first appearance in the new field, but there was nothing I could do except wait and see what happened.

Well, it happened all right. When old No Carrie came up with his head under the neck yoke, all hell broke loose. He started bucking, pulled his tail loose from Geronimo, whirled around, turned the buggy over, and bucking and kicking, he fell down. A man named Forrest Sherman was standing nearby. He piled on No Carrie's head and held him down. Two other fellows soon had Geronimo eared down, and they were all having a lot of fun. They got both horses loose from the buggy, helped me turn the buggy right side up, and began to gather up my stuff.

I had been working on a sermon for the next Sunday while driving along, so my Bible and sermon notes were scattered about. I saw Forrest pick up the Bible, look at me, and glance around at the other fellows. They helped me get the horses hitched to the buggy and when I tied the ponies' tails together again, they asked why. I replied it was for a very good reason. As I got in the buggy Forrest asked where I was going to preach next. I said, "Here." I got in the buggy and took a swing around the town section, where I found a fellow who told me where the Brennands lived. I drove to their house and around to the back of the corral, and that was the last time I ever hitched those crazy little ponies to the buggy.

The next morning I asked if anybody knew of anyone who wanted to trade a good saddle and horse for a team and buggy. Someone thought the banker would like to have the team and buggy as he was sparking a new lady in town, so I went over to the bank and asked him about it. He was interested and asked if the horses were gentle and well broken. I said they were very gentle if he kept their tails tied together. He showed me a good young horse and a good saddle. We traded, but I noticed that on Sunday afternoon when he took the lady out driving, he had a different team hitched to the buggy.

At my first service on Sunday morning, I had a good crowd. Word had gotten around about my spectacular entrance into town and the back rows were filled with cowboys. Forrest Sherman was among them; we became very close friends, and our friendship lasted until his death more than thirty years later. I saw him become an active member of the church and he was one of the main persons to help us get the Cowboy Camp Meeting started on Nogal Mesa.

From Seminole, with packhorse and saddle, I ranged far out across the range country, riding in the roundups, trying to be a hand by day and often preaching in ranch homes, and to men around the campfires. I reached out for two hundred miles, and what a rich and full ministry I enjoyed! In these years, as I rode the wide range country, I preached in many places and made many wonderful friendships that have lasted through all the long years.

Missionary to the Ranch People and Cowboys

AFTER I TRADED that team and buggy for a fine young saddle horse and a comfortable western saddle, a cowboy loaned me a good packhorse. I started out one beautiful May morning on my first trip as a regular commissioned missionary, sent out by the Presbytery of El Paso to present the good news of the Gospel of my Lord and Savior to the ranch people and cowboys. The dream that had started so long ago and faded so many times was really coming true. It seemed to me that morning that it was an exact picture of my boyhood's dream and after riding for some distance meditating on the wonder of it, I was filled with thanksgiving and happiness. I just had to do what I have so often had to do in the presence of God's wonderful blessings. I stopped in the shade of a small mesquite tree, got down on my knees and said once more, "Thank You, dear God, for making my dream come true," and reconsecrated my whole life to Him, to follow that trail wherever it might lead me.

The trail that I started on that morning has led me into many strange and far places. There have been many detours and bypaths, almost every one leading me into some new and wonderful experience. After each detour I have been led back into that main trail to seek fulfillment of my dreams in the service of my Savior.

The trail has led me from Mexico to Canada, from the Atlantic to the Pacific, to so many places where I had very rich experiences of His presence and grace. It has led me a thousand times to lonely and isolated homes out across the great western range country, where I could be of service and help. It has always been with a sense of humility and privilege that I have knocked at the doors of these homes. When the door is opened, I can say to them that I am a minister just passing, then, "How are you? Is all well with you? Are you Christian people? Does a minister ever call? Have you a Sunday School?" Never one single time have I been turned away from a home because of the fact that I am a minister.

As I sometimes walk back along that trail that has become a great highway in memory, and view these homes and the families, it astonishes me to remember how many times I arrived just after some tragedy or some serious illness or deep sorrow. What a great privilege to share with them in their need, to bring a message of hope, to say a prayer with them.

This trail has led me seven times to the platform of the General Assembly in its regular meeting to speak at a popular meeting, presenting the cause of National Missions from San Francisco to Philadelphia. It has led to the great hall of the Academy of Music in Philadelphia where I had the privilege and honor of sharing the platform with the Moderator of the General Assembly before several thousand people as they celebrated the 150th anniversary of the organization of the Presbytery of Philadelphia. It led me to the pulpit of the Old First Presbyterian Church in Pittsburgh, Pennsylvania where I had the honor of speaking at the missionary program as they celebrated the 150th anniversary of their organization.

The trail has led me to a thousand little one-room schoolhouses, where by dim oil lamps I have been privileged to preach the Gospel to a lonely people, hungry for the Good News. It has led me high in the great Rocky Mountain range from Canada to Mexico, to camp with and preach the Gospel to some 17,000 young people who have come to camp with us in different youth conferences, all in temples of God's own making. It has led me into the same country where I have had the joy of telling the ageless story of redeeming love to thousands of ranch families who have gathered to camp for five days of fellowship and worship, spoken of as the cowboy camp meeting.

It has led me ofttimes to walk with friends and loved ones through the valley and shadow of death as I have shared their deep sorrow and loneliness. Too, it has often led me into the green pastures and to tarry beside the still waters, with dear friends in times of joy and happiness.

This trail is one that has been traveled by a humble missionary under a commission from the Board of National Missions. It is a trail that has been traveled for more than a half of a century by that small lad who so many years ago had a beautiful dream and a burning heart. It has led him into a ministry that has been rich and full, far more rewarding than anything else he never could have done.

A Night's Ride Through the Storm

OFTEN I WOULD GO OUT on long trips and be gone sixty or ninety days. I seldom came back on the same horse I started out on. It was not unusual for me to ride hard and long hours. When my horse would begin to be worn out, I would leave him at a ranch, to be picked up at some future date, or just trade him to some cowboy for a fresh one. Sometimes I would get a good one and sometimes a crazy one.

I have ridden some wonderful horses and I have had some real lulus. And I often have been grateful for the good traits even in the worst of them.

One year on the night before Christmas Eve, I found myself preaching in a ranch home about a hundred and twenty miles from my bachelor headquarters. I did want to be home for Christmas Day to get mail and I thought someone might send me a Christmas present. I had been out on this trip for about six weeks. I told the three cowboys who were sharing their quarters in the bunkhouse with me of my desire to get home. They said, "We'll see that you get an early start."

When we got up at four o'clock the next morning there was a dense fog. One of the boys got on the rustling horse

20

and went out to try to find the *remuda* 'the ranch herd of horses'. He came back about daylight and said he could not find anything, the fog was so thick. We got some coffee and talked it over. They had only the one rustling horse, but they did have a pair of wild mules they were breaking to pull the chuck wagon. They decided the other two fellows would saddle a wild mule apiece and go help hunt the remuda.

They roped and saddled those mules and mounted — and what a rodeo we had! Finally after the mules had bucked a while, the boys told me to open the corral gate and let them out in the open country. When I opened the gate, out they went on a dead run with the wild mules bucking and bawling; in a few yards they were out of sight in the fog and I wondered if they would ever get back. I waited a long time and drank a lot of coffee, but after what seemed to me to be hours, I heard them hollering and the horses running. I had the gate open and two of them drove in about thirty head of the remuda. My horse was among them. I roped him and pulled him out to saddle.

One of the fellows looked at the old "piebald, stocking legged" horse I had ridden hard for two days and said, "Heck, you'll never get out of the horse pasture on that outfit." He told the other fellow to catch "Ole High Pockets" for me. "You can ride him all the way to hell and back and he will still be fresh," he said. "Just don't spare him. He can take it." I told them I had a good, fresh horse at the Y.-Bar side camp about sixty miles up the way on my route. "Fine," they said. "Just leave our horse there and tell the boys to throw him back down this way if they have a chance. Old High Pockets is fresh, now ride!"

I did. He was a dandy and sure could cover the country. I rode through the horse pasture at the Y.-Bar and found my Old Nig, fat and fresh. A hurried supper was prepared by the cowboy there while I roped and saddled Old Nig so he could soak a little while I was eating.

Now Old Nig was a wonderful horse with great endurance, but he did have a streak of meanness in him. I mounted, and after he had bucked me off in a big pile of tin cans, much to the amusement of the cowboy watching me, I mounted again and we headed northeast. I liked him for a long, hard ride, especially if it was a night ride, for he would travel in a straight course — particularly if we were heading for the home pasture. He had been raised at Seminole and loved his home grounds.

It was a warm, beautiful Christmas Eve night. The stars were bright and seemed so close. I felt I could almost reach up and touch them. For about an hour we made good time. Then, as though a heavy veil had been pulled across the canopy of the heavens, it became very dark. The storm hit at first with a freezing rain and high wind. The rain froze as it fell and soon Nig's mane was a mat of ice. I reached back and untied my old gum riding slicker off the back of my saddle. This action did not please Nig. He began bucking and by the time I got him stopped and my slicker on, I had lost all sense of direction. It became utterly still and started snowing very hard. I hardly knew which way was up or which way was down and I didn't think he knew much more; but he seemed to know which way he wanted to go so I gave him his head, hoping he would take me to some ranch or camp where I could find shelter. But Nig seemed to have only one thought in mind; to get home.

On through the long winter night and falling snow we traveled, making good time. I didn't know whether we were traveling toward Canada or Mexico, and I thought we should be hitting one or the other for we were covering a lot of ground. If we crossed a trail or road I didn't know it; everything was covered with the fast-falling snow. We crossed many fences, but they meant nothing to me. All I knew was that Nig seemed to know where he was going.

Finally I realized we had to stop. He was completely played out, and so was I. I unsaddled and hobbled him and scraped the snow from the ground. Beneath the snow I found loose sand, still warm from the day before. Putting my head under my saddle, with the saddle blanket under me and the big slicker pulled over me for a cover, I was soon asleep. I had no idea what time it was, nor how far I had ridden, nor where we were.

After a good nap, I woke up and thought I was warm until I crawled out from under the snow. Then my teeth began to chatter and I realized that I was chilled through. Old Nig stood where I had unsaddled him, all humped up and his back covered with snow. I saddled him, wondering which way he would head. For once he didn't throw me off, but just turned around from the way I had him headed and hit a good fast fox trot. In less than a mile we came to a windmill and an old hackberry tree. I could hardly make myself believe what I was seeing; we were within two miles of Seminole, home. Right then I would not have sold Old Nig for any price. He had traveled a straight course through that storm and darkness for sixty miles, carrying me to where we both wanted to be.

I found that Roger Sherman had brought me a big hunk of the finest ranch-killed beef and his mother had sent along a big, beautiful coconut cake. Soon I had a fire made, a pot of coffee, a few pounds of steak and a half-dozen eggs fried. I don't know when food had tasted so good.

And do you know that fresh coconut cake is awfully good for Christmas morning breakfast?

A neighbor had my mail and Christmas presents spread out there on the table. It was a wonderful Christmas.

The Hobbs Story

BACK IN THE EARLY DAYS of my ministry I rode out one day from the little town of Midland, on the western plains of Texas, heading north and west into an area where I had heard that new homestead country had been opened and people were moving in. I didn't ride far that March morning until I saw yonder on the northwestern horizon a dark bank of clouds that meant just one thing at that time of year: one of those western sandstorms was approaching. Soon I rode into the wind, and what a sandstorm it turned out to be! Soon the sun became obscured by the blowing sand and there wasn't anything I could see in any direction but sand. In my wandering through the storm I came to many fences. I carried a pair of wire pliers on my saddle so I could get down and pull off the top wire. My horse, Sandy had been trained to jump over the lower part of the fence, and then I would nail the wire back in place and ride on.

All day long I rode without encountering a single cowboy or finding a single ranch. Late in the night Sandy played out after plowing through the deep sand and facing the wind. I stopped and hobbled him so he could graze. Then I threw my saddle on the ground, put my head up under it, pulled my old gummed slicker up over me for a covering, and had a good night's sleep. When I awoke in the morning the storm was still going strong, for it was one of those three-day blows. For breakfast I had a can of Vienna sausage. I had lost my pocketknife so had to open the can with my spur and the sausages were a little bit scrambled. I had some crushed crackers that I had tied up in that old slicker. But, considering everything I had a good breakfast.

I rode on and about eleven o'clock that morning I came to the first habitation I had seen since leaving home the day before. I found a little one-room adobe store building with a lean-to shed where the family lived. This store and a post office were called Hobbs, New Mexico. I knocked at the door and was greeted by a mother with two or three small children gathered around her. I told her who I was and why I stopped. She gave me a very cordial welcome. We had talked but a minute when she sent one of the children down to the corral to tell her husband that a minister was there. He came in and immediately, as often happened, he said, "How long can you stay? Can we have a preaching service?" And I said, "Sure." So they got on their horses and rode off in different directions to tell their neighbors.

By evening seventeen people had gathered in this little adobe store building. With the women and children sitting around on boxes and the men squatting on their heels, I preached the first sermon that had been preached in that area.

I have never been able to go into one of these communities and realize that I am standing there to preach the first sermon ever preached in that place without beginning to dream dreams and to have a hope and a prayer that it may be the beginning of a great work of the building of God's Kingdom in that place.

After the service we had coffee and sandwiches and then I remember one of the ladies saying, "It isn't very late and it doesn't matter what time we get home, would it be asking too much to ask you to preach another sermon for us?" I said "No, I'll be glad to preach." And then it was that old story: "When can you come back? Won't you come back soon?" I said, "I'll be passing back this way sometime next year and I'll stop."

Well, I went back to Hobbs from time to time and we could no longer get into the little adobe house. We went down to a grove of cottonwood trees by an old windmill and we held three services a day. The people would bring their lunches and we would have dinner on the ground, and what wonderful times we had.

Then there came a day, in 1928 I guess it was, when oil was discovered in that area and almost overnight Hobbs became a wild, roaring oil town. Uncle John Henry went there with me and we stayed for two months on one occasion. We preached on the street corners; we preached in half-completed buildings, or wherever we could find a place to hold a service. Soon a little church was organized and a chapel was erected.

Then many years later, some thirty-five years after my first visit, Mrs. Hall and I stood one May morning in a beautiful sanctuary of a new church, with Sunday School rooms and all equipment, which I was to dedicate. The man who introduced me that morning, the pastor of the church, was our son James. This was truly a dream coming true and a prayer answered. And Hobbs today has one of the outstanding churches of the Synod of New Mexico.

In November, 1959, Mrs. Hall and I were invited by the session of the Hobbs Church to come down and spend the Sunday with them. As we walked into the sanctuary, the first thing we saw was a beautiful new stained glass window depicting the Great Commission, "Go Ye Into All the World and Preach the Gospel." Around the edges of the window we saw a series of panels depicting the life and the work of the Sunday School missionary. There is one of the missionary with his saddle horse and his packhorse making camp. There is another of the little chapel and people coming in and out. One shows the schoolhouse with the young people gathered. One is of the Sunday School missionaries gathered for a retreat out in a beautiful pine grove. And one shows the camp meeting tent and scenes of the camp meeting. Then down in the center it says, "In appreciation of Ralph Hall and others like him."

It was truly a wonderful experience and I will always be grateful to the church at Hobbs for this manifestation of their love and affection.

Having Some Fun

DURING MY STAY AT SEMINOLE I roomed in the manse, batching mostly but eating often in the Brennand home where the schoolteachers boarded. I don't know what the cowboys would have done for dates, sweethearts or wives had it not been for the young ladies who came out to teach in the small country schools.

I got into the habit of making my headquarters in the homes and boardinghouses across the great range country where the schoolteachers lived.

In those days we had to make our own fun, such as house parties, hay rides, or attending cattle roundups. It was a time for large practical jokes, sometimes going pretty far. I guess I played my part of them, but I was often the fall guy.

In one of the places where I preached quite often, about thirty-five miles from headquarters, I met an attractive and delightful young lady who was visiting her sister for the summer. She was from Kentucky, was wild about the West and very much interested in the cowboys. I soon began to make detours on my regular trips to stop for a call on her. Sometimes I made the seventy-mile round trip on horseback just to spend an evening with her.

I learned that she had a birthday coming up and asked for the privilege of calling on her on her birthday. I knew I should take a gift, but I didn't have anything that would be appropriate. A little while before her birthday, I was not too far from Midland where they carried fine candy in stock. I rode about twenty-five miles extra to pick up the finest I could buy. It was in the winter, so I could keep it in good shape. I carried it home in my gum slicker tied back of my saddle, and stored it in an unused and unheated bedroom on a high shelf in the closet.

Now every once in a while some of the schoolteachers would go over to the manse and give my bachelor quarters a good cleaning. They had just been over to do the usual cleaning when the day came for the thirty-five mile ride to deliver the candy. I never suspected they had known about the candy or the birthday coming up, but they found that candy and decided to play a real joke on me. They carefully unwrapped the box, took out the candy, made adobe mud balls of the same size and filled the box, rewrapping it so well no one could tell it had ever been touched.

Well, the joke worked all too completely. I didn't know just how to go about presenting a lovely lady a box of candy, but after visiting a little while I suggested a stroll in the moonlight — though the moon was pretty dim. As we came out of the yard where my horse was tied, I made as if I had just remembered something and led her over to the horse, untied the old gum slicker and handed her the candy. She seemed so very pleased, saying it had been so long since she had really had any good candy. It was light enough for her to see the brand on the box. She exclaimed with great joy, "Oh, my very favorite. How lovely."

I thought things were going well. She managed to get the wrappings off and said, "Now you must have the first piece," and pushed it to me. I took the first piece all right, but the minute I touched it I knew something was wrong. Before I could do anything she stuck a whole big ball of adobe mud in her mouth. She slammed the whole box in my face saying, "That was a dirty trick! Good night and good-bye, Mr. Cowboy!"

It was, too. It took me a long time and many jokes to get even with those pesky schoolteachers.

In one of the communities where some land had been opened for homesteading, a good many families had moved in with lots of children and there was a great need to add a high school. Two new teachers for the high school came from the East. Their boarding place also became one of my favorite stopping places, where I could always look forward to a pleasant evening. I came in late one cold evening from several days in the saddle, tired and hungry, riding hard to make it in time for supper. I had to open a gate near the town, and as I was shutting the gate, I saw an old horned toad frog. I reached down and picked him up thinking he might come in handy in some way, and stuck him in my mackinaw coat pocket.

When I arrived at the boardinghouse, I found everyone was in the dining room eating supper. As I paused in the hallway I noticed a big hat and coat rack, and on it the large, heavy coat of one of the high school teachers. She was the type who simply could not stand any kind of insect, fly, or bug around. If a candle bug got in her hair she would have a fit. So I just dropped the frog in her pocket. Then I went on in, receiving a hearty welcome from the group at the table.

They told me they were so glad I had made it in time to go with them to a high school program, the big event of the year. Soon they were saying, "Everyone hurry or we'll be late."

Before I had time to think about the frog, we were on our way, all walking in a group, jostling each other. I knew I had to get that frog out of the teacher's pocket for she was to have charge of the program. I tried to walk close to her, kept trying to get my hand in her pocket, but nothing doing. She commanded me to keep my hands out of her

30

pocket. Before I could do anything we were going up the stairs to the auditorium where the program was to be held. The hall was already crowded. I insisted on taking her coat, caring for it while she did the program, but she said, "No, it is cold in here and I'll keep it on."

The first number on the program was a piano duet by two of the high school girls, and this teacher was turning the pages for them. Several times I saw her slip her hand down a little way in that pocket, and each time I almost had a stroke for I knew if she found that frog she would have a conniption fit. Just as the girls finished their piece the crowd broke out in a loud clapping. She turned to walk toward the center of the stage — and then it happened.

As she shoved her hand to the bottom of the pocket there was a wild scream: "SNAKE!" She began tearing at her coat and running down the steps from the platform. I was sitting at the end of the aisle and as she came by I grabbed her and literally tore her coat off. Some women stopped her then and were trying to find out what had happened. While all that was going on I got that frog in my pocket, threw her coat away, worked my way to the side of the room where there was a partly open window, and gave Mr. Frog his freedom.

Everyone thought she had lost her mind. When she calmed down, she told them there was a snake in her coat pocket. They searched her coat but of course found nothing. Almost everyone knew how afraid she was of any insect or snake. She did have a pair of buckskin gloves in the pocket, so they were able to convince her that a glove was what she had touched.

Boy, that was a close one. I hope she never reads this.

In one community the people had built a community hall where they had all kinds of programs, dancing parties and so forth. We also used it for worship services on Sunday afternoons when I could get there. Some very large wasps had built their nest on the high ceiling, and sometimes when we heated the building with the big wood stove the wasps would drop down from the ceiling.

One cold December afternoon two of the schoolteachers were to sing a duet in the service. These two teachers were just back of my chair. When I stood up to read the scripture before the ladies were to sing, one of these old wasps fell into my chair. As I was ready to step back and sit down, one of the teachers started to knock him off the chair, but the other teacher grabbed her hand and let nature take its course.

No one except these two ladies knew about the wasp. When I bent to sit down, stretching my trousers as tight as could be, I sat down on that feller and received the greatest shock, the worst instant and intense pain I think I ever felt. Of course I didn't sit long. I came up several feet, I guess, and slammed my hand back where it hurt. Then I proceeded to step on the wasp with an apology to the congregation, although most of them already sensed what happened.

I once more announced the ladies would sing. I knew one of these ladies was a terrible giggler, and that if she got tickled she just could not control herself. Well, they started to sing, but after a few notes, one of them began running down the long aisle and out the door. We had to take a few minutes to get settled down, with a word from me about the whole affair.

I had a hard time preaching my sermon — because for one thing, the laughing girl had gone to her car which was parked in front of a large window in my clear view. I could not help but watch her as she rocked back and forth, doubled up in laughter.

When going out on long trips I usually took a packhorse so I could take a camping outfit. However, through summer I did not always take an extra horse, but just what I could carry on my saddle. At night the ground was warm, often almost hot, and I had my gum slicker for a cover.

One of the big jobs was shaving. I had never heard of a safety razor or shaving cream in tubes. I just took along the old straight razor and strop, and a cake of hand soap. I would stop at a dirt tank or windmill, lather my face with soap, strop my razor, and shave without a mirror. My skin must have been tough in those days, and it's a good thing it was.

I remember one night when it was raining, a homestead family who lived in a dugout (just a hole dug in the ground with a gable roof going from the top of the ground up) insisted that I sleep inside. The family consisted of a mother and daughter, and a son about my age. They had two double beds in the room. Mother and daughter slept in one bed at one end of the room, and the son and I at the other.

After supper we were sitting around visiting. I saw a big bull snake crawling along where the ground met the roof, just about the height of our heads as we sat in the chairs. The boy reached over and stuck his cigarette against the critter, which just crawled on, dropped down on the bed, and slithered under it.

I asked, "Aren't you going to put him out?" The mother replied, "No. That old thing stays in here all the time. He keeps the rats out. If he crawls over your bed, just don't pay him any mind."

It was not a very comfortable night.

A Fine Preacher

OFTEN THERE WOULD BE PEOPLE who wanted to be baptized or join one of the little churches where I preached, or would want their babies baptized or have a communion service. Of course, not being ordained, I could not do any of these things for them. Every time the presbytery would meet I had a lot of requests for an ordained minister to come to do these things for us. Usually the presbytery would say to Louis Cunningham, "You go help him out."

Louis got tired of making these long trips on horseback. On one occasion when I needed help, the moderator turned to Louis Cunningham and said, "Will you do it?" Louis said, "No. You should ordain him so he can do it himself, or some of you fellows should get out and learn what it is like."

The moderator asked, "Who will volunteer?" There was an awful silence. Then Dr. Houston W. Lowery, a minister who wore the cloth with great dignity and who for health reasons had just come from a large church in Ohio to be pastor of the church at Carlsbad, spoke up. "This sounds very interesting to me. If I would be acceptable, I'll be glad to go."

The moderator replied, "Make your arrangements with Ralph. You have the job."

I thought it would be wonderful to have Dr. Lowery come and stay five days with me and preach twice each day. It would give the people an opportunity to hear some real preaching, for Dr. Lowery was a great pulpit man.

I made arrangements with Dr. Lowery to come two weeks later. He was very much excited about the prospect of getting out in the country and spending these days with ranch and homestead people. He was to take the stage (an old Cadillac car) out east for about sixty miles, then transfer to a mail hack and ride it to a certain mailbox. There I would meet him with a saddle horse for the last seven miles to the homestead where we were to spend the night. I told him if for any reason I was not there by the time he arrived, to have the mailman put him off to wait for me.

I had a long ride that day and had stopped at a roundup where they were shorthanded so I helped them for a while. I knew by the time I left the outfit I would have to hurry to meet Dr. Lowery.

I had written a family who lived nearby that I wanted to pick up an extra horse and saddle for Dr. Lowery. When I got there the lady was very much upset; her husband had not returned home as he had planned and all the saddle horses were gone. But, she said, "There is a little old bronc horse out there in the trap. He has been ridden a few times. You are welcome to use him. There's a saddle in the barn."

I went out and roped the bronc, drug him in and saddled him, and hit a lope for the mailbox. I knew I was late.

When I got within sight of the mailbox way out there on the prairie, I could see Dr. Lowery walking up and down the road. The sun was almost down and not a thing could be seen in any direction from where he was walking. He was about ready to take off — for somewhere — so he was extra glad to see me.

I had told him to pack very light as we would be traveling horseback and couldn't carry much.

I guess for him he had packed light but he had a pretty big suitcase. I told him he could ride Old Nig, my horse, and I would try to ride that little bronc. Nig was a good horse but had a very tender mouth; if you pulled too hard on him he would rear up and had been known to fall over backward. I gave Dr. Lowery the suitcase and told him he could carry it in front of him for the short distance. I then mounted the bronc and things picked up.

The bronc started to buck, and bumped into Nig. Dr. Lowery dropped the suitcase and hauled back on the reins. I saw Nig rear up and was afraid he was going over backward, so I jumped off my horse and rushed over to get hold of Nig's head. Dr. Lowery was squalling as loud as he could to Nig to "WHOA!" I got the horse quieted down and Dr. Lowery pacified. Then I told him I would have to use his horse to catch mine. I had a hard time catching that little old bronc, for he was heading for home, but finally I roped him and brought him back. I got Dr. Lowery mounted again and started to hand him the suitcase.

"Throw it away," he said. "This horse has all he will carry. Don't think I'll live to use it anyway."

There was a little narrow gate nearby, made so school children could ride their horses through it. I tied the suitcase loosely to one of the gateposts and knew the little pony would have to get close enough for me to grab it as we rode past. I was able to grab it as we dashed through, and we were on our way.

We cut quite a pair of figures with Dr. Lowery (a very large, heavy man) dressed in his black double-breasted suit and derby hat, riding on Nig, and me on the little bronc that would weigh about six hundred pounds, and the big suitcase.

The next evening we had our first service in a little schoolhouse that was filled and overflowing, with people looking in the windows. We had no musical instrument to help in the music and we only had a few hymnbooks. We had no pulpit, just the low desk the teacher used. There

36

were two kerosene lamps hanging, one on each wall. They didn't give much light, and Dr. Lowery always read his sermons.

I introduced him and told people what a great preacher he was. He was, indeed, an outstanding speaker. But for the first time in his life he found himself without a pulpit to place his notes on, without a choir, pipe organ or pews. I had not realized how difficult it was going to be for him to preach in such circumstances. He walked over to the light on the wall that was hanging high so as to spread the light as far as possible, and managed to get the Scripture read. Then he got out his small notebook to read his sermon. With that dim light, high up, and with his bifocal glasses, it was almost impossible for him to read. I don't think I have ever felt as sorry for anyone. The perspiration poured off his forehead and down his face. I never wanted so much to help a fellow in my life.

There lived in the community a dear old couple who were especially kind to me and always called me "their boy." We were to spend the night with them in their little two-room cottage. The center partition in their house only went as high as the walls and as far as sound was concerned we might as well all have been in the same room.

Dr. Lowery and I were in one bed and their bed in the other room was against the partition wall. I think we were all slow getting off to sleep.

Far in the night when I am sure they thought we were sound asleep, we heard her say to her husband, "How did you like old Dr. Lowery's sermon?" He replied, "That was all right." She went on to say she didn't think he knew much about preaching or he wouldn't have to read his sermons. He told her that Dr. Lowery had not been preaching in little schoolhouses and had always had good light to read by, and that many great preachers read their sermons.

Finally, she asked, "Now Daddy, honestly and down deep in your heart, hadn't you rather hear our boy preach?"

He replied, "Oh yes, of course. Now go to sleep."

I had started to cough and make sort of a noise early in the conversation to stop them, but Dr. Lowery had shushed me and whispered, "Don't; just listen." He shook the bed for a long time laughing.

The next morning he said, "Let's take a walk right now." He had his Bible and sermon notebook. We walked out in the pasture where we found a mesquite bush and sat down in the shade. "Now," he said, "You are going to do the preaching. I just can't. I have never preached without reading my sermon, and I cannot do it by that light. That was the worst failure last night I ever had . . ."

I told him I just could not, as I only had a few sermons and had preached all of them there, and it was not easy for me to get a sermon. "Here's a book full of them," he said. "I'll help you. I'll pray for you. I'll say, 'amen,' I'll do anything. You look through and maybe you can get a suggestion or an idea. Use anything you can find here. I will take the morning service but never again at night by that dim light."

So I spent the next five days out in the brush, and preached each evening and he in the morning. His daytime preaching was as fine as anyone could ask, and mine at night was certainly better because of his notes and his help.

Study and Ordination

THE PRESBYTERY SUGGESTED that I take some courses of study when I could, and suggested Dr. Charles Downing and Dr. Lowery as instructors. I rode horseback twice a month, some two hundred miles each way, to sit at the feet of these two wonderful, Godly men as they crammed theology, church history and church government down my throat. "If you are not able to go back to school and will study hard," the people at presbytery said, "some day we can ordain you."

Very much to my surprise, in the spring of 1916, I was told to come to presbytery prepared for examination and ordination. Presbytery spent two days examining and instructing me, and the third day they ordained me to the Gospel ministry. I will never forget those three days.

Dr. Downing and Dr. Lowery insisted that the presbytery give me a thorough examination, especially in Bible, theology, church history, church government, and sacraments. I will always be grateful to those two fine men who gave of their time and love out of their busy lives. They were very kind and understanding and did not want me to feel that I was just sliding by this great event in a minister's life.

I had to preach a formal sermon before presbytery and

39

they commented on it very frankly with many suggestions. I also had to write a sermon on a designated passage of Scripture. I assured the presbytery I would never seek a large pulpit but wanted to give myself in a ministry to the ranch people in small churches and scattered communities of the west. This is where my ministry has been, and no one could ask for a fuller, richer life.

The First Ford

THE TIME CAME when the presbytery felt I should have a Model T Ford so I could cover more ground and increase the extent of my ministry, so I bought my first car. The dealer drove me around the block, stepped out and said, "You're on your own." I was afraid to stop the outfit for fear I would never be able to start it again, so I just headed out of Barstow for Seminole.

I often had to cross the Monahans sand — a barren, desert kind of area, and always had a time. I found an old five-gallon oil can and carried it full of water. I would take my eighteen-foot tarp off my bedroll and when I would get stuck, I would put it down in the sand and go eighteen feet at a time. I would let a part of the air out of my tires to help the car get traction, then I would have to pump them up again with an old hand pump. I guess I wished for Old Nig many times in those spots.

That Ford played a lot of tricks on me, as pesky as some of the horses had done. I remember one cold, dark night traveling from Carlsbad to Pecos. It was not much of a road, and went along close to the Pecos River most of the way. An awful sandstorm was blowing. There were many gates to open, so I would have to get out, open the gate, get back in and drive through, then get out again and shut the gate. When I came to one of these gates I was traveling with the wind to my back. I got out, opened the gate and drove through as usual. Then I went back to shut the gate. The lights were on a magneto and when the motor stopped, the lights would go out. I had throttled the motor down too much, and while I was struggling with the gate — it was a very tough one — the motor stopped and the lights of course went out. After some time I got the gate closed and turned around to feel for my car. It was gone, plumb gone.

I could not see three feet ahead of me. Soon, not only was the Ford lost but so was I. I wandered around for awhile and could find neither the road nor the car, so I decided I had better wait until morning. I had on a heavy overcoat so I just sat down, pulled the overcoat up over my head, and waited for daylight. I thought that when it got light I would see the old Ford right nearby. When it finally began to get light I could see a long way across the prairie — but no Ford. The wind had covered all tracks. I had no idea which way it went. Finally I walked over to the river and after following the bank for some distance I found the old Ford, right side up where it had gone over the edge and down there in the brush. I tried to find some place where it was not too steep, so I could drive the Ford back up on level ground. I could not find a good place and was digging down the bank hoping I could slope it enough to get the car out, when a Spanish man with a wagon and team happened along. He tied on to me and pulled me out, and I began to wonder if I should hobble that car like I would a horse.

One other time, just before Christmas, I had been out in a very isolated area to visit an old cowboy and his wife who were staying in a line camp. It was warm and dry as I went in, but as I left I found the roads covered with snow. When I went to see these folks they always wanted to give me something, so when I was ready to leave the man put a steak and a ten-pound pail of lard in my chuck box.

42

The road was a rocky trail and with the deep snow I couldn't see the high rocks. I hit one going downhill at a pretty good clip. It knocked a hole in the car's crankcase and soon all the oil was gone. I decided I would build a fire and eat that good steak the cowboy had given me, and think things over. After eating, and drinking a lot of good camp coffee, I got under the Ford to see how much damage I had done. I saw that the crankcase would not hold any oil, even if I had any. As I said, it was just before Christmas and friends had sent me candy and chewing gum for children in that isolated region. I was looking through the car to see if I could find anything that might patch that hole enough so it would hold oil until I could get somewhere. I knew it would be a long walk any way I went, and cars seldom traveled over that rough road.

Then I saw the box of chewing gum, a whole carton of it. Would it hold? I thought it worth a try. But what would I do for oil? As I looked at the chuck box I saw that bucket of lard. Would it work? I didn't know, but I had to do something.

I sat down and began chewing gum. Do you know how much gum there is in a whole carton? I can tell you now that it is a lot if you chew it up in one sitting.

When the big ball was finally chewed, I took an old pair of pants and cut off a leg, got under the car, put the gum over the ragged hole, and poked it in tight. I took bailing wire (I always carried some for repairs; it is surprising what you can do with a piece of bailing wire on a broken-down Model T Ford), tied a piece in each of the four corners and, putting the patch of cloth over the chewing gum, tied the wire to the various nuts and bolts and twisted them tight to hold that patch in place. I put the lard on the fire to melt. While it was boiling hot, I poured it in the crankcase, jumped in, and headed out.

Well, it worked. When I got to a filling station, I drained it out at once while it was still hot, then washed the crankcase out good with kerosene. I saved myself a long walk and did no damage to the motor, but I don't recommend that kind of repair job unless you really like chewing gum.

The Old F. L. Y. Bar Ranch

I HAD HEARD a lot about the old F. L. Y. Bar Ranch and had wanted to visit the cowboys there but had not gotten around to it until I heard they were having a big roundup on the southwest corner of the outfit. So, I saddled and packed my outfit and headed out. I arrived there just as they were ready for supper. I rode in and said, "Hi, fellows. How are things?" The foreman said, "Turn your horses loose and join us," so I got in the chuck line and made myself at home.

I had heard that some of the riders were a pretty tough bunch and I wondered if any of them would know me. I always like to stay around a new outfit for a little while before telling them I am a preacher, not because I am ashamed of what I am but so that they will get to know me just as a man. I looked down the line and saw no familiar faces.

Just after supper the boss asked me if I would mind taking a turn on night guard, because they were shorthanded and the big steers had been very restless and wanted to run at night. I told him I'd be glad to do it. I took the last guard and next morning as they were catching their horses for the day, the foreman asked me if I would like to ride with them. I told him I thought I would stay around a day or so and would be glad to help. "You can ride Old Apple," he said.

Now I had heard more about Old Apple than I had about the outfit I was to ride with, and if I had known Old Apple was in that remuda I might not have been there. But I made as if I had never heard of him and threw my saddle on him, thinking to myself, "I have been bucked off before and expect to be again, so what difference does it make?" Two of the fellows eared him down when I was ready to mount, each of them taking an ear between his teeth.

I did not stay long in that saddle. I made a good landing, much to the amusement of the gang. As I got up I said, "Bring him back. I want to try him again." The boss answered, "Better just turn him loose and we'll catch you one of the children's ponies."

"You gave him to me," I said, "and I want another try at him." That time, by some miracle, I stayed on. When he had tried all of his tricks, he stopped bucking and stuck out his long neck and headed for the open range on a dead run. I knew I had him.

I had gotten quite a way from the roundup ground when the boss caught up with me. He said, "Well, you rode him. Now go back to the remuda and get you a horse and come and catch us for the drive." I knew I was not supposed to ride Old Apple; they just kept him to back off any new cowboy who came along. So I said, "No, you gave me a horse to ride and I'm going to ride him." He tried to persuade me to get another horse, but I had made up my mind, that second time I got on him, that if I could stay on I would give that critter a day's ride he would not soon forget.

They showed me the country they were going to cover in the drive that day and it was a big country, reaching out to the very distant hills on the horizon. I worked around until I was on the outside and would have to cover more ground than anyone else. And what a ride I gave that hoss.

46

When we threw our drives into the main herd at noon, all the other cowboys caught fresh horses. They tried to get me to change but I said, "Old Apple is still going strong." The boss was not there or I am sure I could not have gotten away on him. I came across the boss that afternoon and he sure did bawl me out. I brought Old Apple in that evening on my spurs and if he should still be alive I am sure he still remembers that day's ride, as I do.

I rode two more days with them, making it a point to ride with as many different men as I could so that I could get to know them. They in turn accepted me as just another cowboy riding chuck line. The second afternoon I rode with the boss we found we had mutual friends; I got to know him by his first name. So as we were unsaddling our horses and catching the night horses, I walked over to him and said, "Bob, I am a preacher and I am wondering if I could talk to the boys tonight after supper for a little while."

He said, "The hell you are."

"Sure am," said I.

"Well, I guess there is no law against it," he said.

He didn't say anything to the other fellows until all were through eating. Then: "Some of you fellows bring up some wood and pile it on the fire. We have something special in camp tonight."

He told them to bring up their bedrolls and sit. When they were all settled and had their Bull Durham cigarettes going, he called me and said, "Come over here." Then to the group he said, "Fellows, this guy is a preacher, or at least he says he is." They nudged each other and haw-hawed.

I said, "That's right, fellows." I dug down and pulled out a little Testament from my chap pocket.

When they saw that Testament, every hat came off, every cigarette went out of their mouths and they sat up very reverently. I said, "Suppose you all join me in singing a Gospel song. Let us sing 'What A Friend We Have in Jesus.'"

I thought everyone would know it but for that first stanza we had the worst solo the coyotes ever heard. Then I read the second stanza from the small hymnbook I had and said, "Come on, let's all sing." They did, and I could hardly get them stopped.

I read a passage of Scripture and said, "Let us all bow our heads and say a prayer." At this they did something I never expected them to do: Every one of them got down on his knees, and when I started the prayer they took it up and repeated it all the way through after me. I won't ever forget that moment when I glanced out and saw this group of cowboys kneeling there by their bedrolls, with their heads bowed. I think the reason is that about all they knew of saying a prayer was repeating a child's prayer at a Christian mother's knee.

I stayed five days longer at their earnest request.

On the last evening I said to the cowboys, "It has been wonderful to ride and work with you fellows, to get to know you as men and to talk to you these evenings here around the fire about my Lord and His love and concern for each of you. I cannot stay longer. In the morning I must leave early. I don't know when I will see you fellows again, but I am sure our paths will cross, for I know you are not leaving the range country — and neither am I. But after riding and working with you for the week and preaching each evening, I can't leave without asking you to accept my Lord and my Christ as your personal Savior and asking you to become Christian men." Then I told them what it meant to me to be a Christian man, explaining the plan of salvation to them as I understood it. I said, "You don't have to be in a big church building with big crowds of people, but you can give your heart and life to Christ right now and here in this little group — out here under the stars. Christ is here. I have heard the whispering of His voice in the beauty and glory of this quiet place. Some of you have told me of your problems, of your great concerns. I know my Lord can and will help you if you will accept Him as your

Savior. I know that He in His great love will follow you all the days of your life. He will never let you go alone. I am talking to each of you as man to man. If any of you fellows want to take that step tonight, just come over here and stand on this side of the fire with me."

There was a long moment of absolute silence. The only sound was way over across the hills where I could hear the lonely howling of a coyote. Then seven of this group of cowboys came over, shook hands and stood by my side.

Then a good-night prayer was said as I tried to commend each one of them to my God's will, love, and care. I talked for awhile longer with the little group of seven and advised them to join a church. We said good night and went to our bedrolls.

After some time I heard footsteps approaching my bed. Then a voice, "Preacher, are you asleep?" I replied, "No. Come on over and sit down." He sat down and said, "Some of us have been talking. We really meant what we said and did tonight. When a man does what we did tonight, don't you do something more — well, like baptizing them, taking them into the church?" I said, "Yes." He said, "Can't you do that for us out here tonight?" I said I could not take them into the church. He said, "But couldn't you at least baptize us?" I thought of one other as a new child of God who had said, "Here is water. Why not baptize me?" So I said, "Yes, if you really want me to and if you will promise to join the church the first opportunity you have." I got out of my bedroll, dressed, pulled on my boots, and walked back with him to the chuck wagon. There we found the others waiting. I talked with them some more and asked them if they really wanted me to baptize them. They said they did. I took a tin cup from the chuck box, drew a cup of water from the barrel, and walked back to where those seven cowboys stood with their heads bowed and bared. A full moon had risen high over the eastern hills. The glory of God seemed to hover about the old chuck wagon and these stalwart, humble, newly redeemed men. From the

49

battered tin cup I baptized each one, an experience, a night, I will never, never forget.

Once more back to my bedroll, and a little later, footsteps and a voice again:

"Preacher, are you asleep? It is Ed. I'm sorry to disturb you but I wonder if you would do something for me."

"Sure. What can I do?"

"I have a wonderful, Christian mother living back east of here about three hundred miles. I have broken her heart a hundred times. I know she has shed many a tear over me and I'm sure she has never gone to sleep a single night without saying a prayer for me. Would you write her a letter and tell her what I did tonight, and that when I get home this winter I want to join a church with her? You can explain it better than I can. I know it would make her mighty happy. Tell her I really mean it."

I said, "Sure, Ed. I'll be happy to write to her."

"Then would it be asking too much to ask you to write another letter? Back there is a mighty fine young woman, pretty too, who has consented to be my wife. She is a wonderful Christian and asked me and begged me to become a Christian. I told her someday I would. Will you write and tell her for me that I'm coming to claim her soon and that I'll be a real Christian husband to her? Just one more thing. I have a brother who is one of the best men the Lord ever made, but he just simply hates preachers. I don't know why, but he does. He lives up in the north country on the Big Piney. His name is Frank. You know, I believe if you could spend a little time with him before he knew you were a preacher, like you did with us here on the roundup, you could win him. The Lord knows he needs help. He is passing through deep waters, bogged down in all kinds of trouble. If you ever get that far up north, try to see him. Be sure you don't let him know you're a preacher until you have ridden and worked with him for a good while. He has a pretty big spread."

50

I told him if I ever got near his place I sure would look him up.

I was a very humble and happy man when I said good-bye, long before daybreak the next morning, to this group of cowboys. I think such men have more real nobility of character than any group of people I know in all the world. It was five years later, after I had secured an old Model T Ford, that I was asked to do some work in the north country Ed Adams had spoken about.

It was late November and I was to visit a mining town over the great mountain range. I was heading up that way hoping I would be able to get across the mountains before night came and before a storm broke, as it looked like it might do anytime. But I had all kinds of trouble with the old Ford that day. Five flat tires had to be pulled off, tubes patched with mastic and cement and pumped up by hand because there were no spares those days. By midafternoon it began snowing and was piling up fast. I crossed the Big Piney and thought of Frank Adams, Ed's brother, and said to myself that I would sure try and find him soon. By 7:00 P.M. the snow was getting deep and I began to look for a sheltered place where I might camp.

Suddenly I saw a mailbox by the road, and backed up the old Ford to see if I could see a name by the dim lights. Printed on the box was "Frank Adams," and looking off down the valley I saw a dim light. Whether this was Ed's brother or not, I decided this was a good time to visit.

I drove close to the house; he had seen the lights of the car, had the gate open, and shouted a greeting and said, "Drive right on into the barn."

As I got out he came up and said, "Frank Adams is the name" and I said, "Ralph Hall here" being careful not to put any "Reverend" on it.

"Glad to have you. It looks like a big storm coming on." He picked up my bag and we walked together to the house. He remarked, "You're just in time for supper. We don't see many people out here and are always glad to welcome company." He opened the door and shouted to his wife to put on another plate — "we have company." She came in from the kitchen and her face beamed as she exclaimed, "Why it's Brother Hall."

I never hated to hear that word "Brother" so badly in my whole life. He dropped my bag like it was something hot and walked over to the other side of the room, picked up a paper and began turning through it. His wife, I discovered, had been visiting her sister when I had preached in a schoolhouse near her sister's family ranch. They had all been at the service when we had organized a Sunday School. So Mrs. Adams wanted to talk, to know how the new Sunday School was coming along.

We ate an almost silent supper. Then we sat around the family living room beside a blazing fire in the big fireplace. Disappointment and boredom showed on the old boy's face. He had been looking forward to talking cattle, marketing, rodeos, and his guest turned out to be a damn preacher.

Mrs. Adams was just bubbling over, telling me how much it meant to her sister and her family to have me preach for them and get a Sunday School started. About all she got out of me was "uh-huh" and "uh-uh." I got as much interested in looking at pictures in a magazine as Frank was in turning through his paper. She got busy with her tatting or something of that kind; the teen-age daughter was busy with her schoolwork; it was a pretty dull evening.

Presently old Frank threw down his paper and said he was tired and sleepy and was going to bed. He glanced over my way with a look of disgust on his face and said, "When you get ready to go to bed, go upstairs and take the first room on the right." I said, "I'm sleepy" and picked up my bag and went on up the stairs.

I could hear the wind roaring and looked out the window and saw that it was snowing hard. A regular blizzard was raging. I thought to myself that I hoped I would not get snowed in here.

The next morning about four o'clock I heard the family

stirring around downstairs so I got dressed and went down. I could hear them talking in the kitchen as he helped her prepare breakfast. I had noticed that the snow was piled as high as the windowsill, and I heard him grumbling and growling about it: "This would be my luck. If I could have had one more day I could have gotten those four hundred calves down off the mountain. Now I guess I'll lose half of them. I would give fifty dollars for a good cowhand today."

She got very bold and said, "Maybe Mr. Hall could help you. I heard him talking to my brother-in-law about working in roundups." He said, "Who ever heard of a damn preacher doing anything?"

"Maybe you could get one of the Eperson boys to help," she said.

And he said, "They have as many cattle out as I have. No chance."

Finally we gathered around the table for breakfast. He growled at me and said, "Bless it," meaning the food. I did, wondering if he heard me and what that day would bring.

As we finished breakfast he finally spoke to me again: "Hall, did you ever ride a horse?"

I told him I had ridden some. Then he told me he had had these yearlings up on the mountain and knew the storm had scattered them. He said, "Would you help me? It will be a long, hard two-days ride, but I'll pay you well. You won't have to do much. I'll gather them and throw them down in the valley and you can just keep them together and drifting down the canyon."

I told him I would be very pleased to help him out. As we went down to the corral he told his wife to pack some grub and that we would not get back until late the next night.

As we got to the barn he lighted the old lantern hanging on the wall and went over to the saddle rack where there were several saddles. "Pick out one," he said. "I think the one on the end is the best."

I thanked him and told him I had my own saddle and outfit in the car. I went over and got my saddle, spurs and chaps, and threw them down in the lantern light. He glanced at them, came over and picked up the chaps and turned the saddle over for a good look, then remarked, "That is a darn good outfit." I wasn't ashamed of it, for the cowboys have always seen that I had the very best in that line.

There were about twenty-five saddle horses milling around in the roping corral. I got my rope off the saddle and walked with him to the barn door. He stepped out and roped himself a horse. I stood there with my loop ready. He said, "What's the matter, getting cold feet?"

I said, "I am ready to do business when you tell me what horse to rope." I knew he should tell me what horse to catch. He said, "Oh, catch that buckskin right there, the one on the outside."

You could not tell a buckskin from a roan in the darkness, but I stepped out and happened to make a good catch. I pulled him into the light at the barn door and realized that I had quite a horse on the end of my rope. I picked up my bridle to put it on him. Frank rushed over and said, "Here, I'll bridle him for you. He's pretty shy."

I said, "I think I can make it," but he went over and bridled the horse. He said, "Watch him when you throw your saddle on. He is kinder skittish." I got my saddle on. After getting to his head and pulling the cinch tighter, Frank bustled up and pushing me aside said, "I'll top him off for you. That old outfit bucks a little sometimes when it's cold."

I foolishly bristled up and said to him, "Well, if you want to ride this horse, take him and I'll catch me another."

He said, "Oh well, go ahead and break your fool neck; who cares."

So with a prayer that the Lord would help me stay on top, I mounted. That horse and I caused quite a commo-

54

tion as he buckled into the rest of the remuda, and to my surprise I was still on top when he quit bucking. Without any more comment Frank said, "Catch that little black there in the corner and put that packsaddle on him while I grab our grub."

When he came back with the sack of grub and we had tied it and a sack of oats on the packsaddle, we started out. The wind had piled the snow up in deep drifts. He said, "Follow me and we will take turns about breaking the trail."

We started climbing out of the valley to the high mesa. Often the snow was up to our stirrups. Nothing was said; I was determined that I could be just as silent as he could and I was not going to force any conversation. After we had gone quite a long distance he rode his horse out of the trail and said, "Get up here and break trail for a while." I rode past him and we went on our way.

About ten o'clock he whistled a few bars of some tune, looked up at the sky and around and said, "Hall, do you suppose it is going to snow all day, or will it clear about noon?" I said, "I don't know and I don't care."

About 2:00 P.M. he said, "Well it is past noon. Do you want to eat a bite? We could make a can of coffee." I said, "You are running this outfit." He said, "Keep riding."

Late in the afternoon we topped out over a high ridge and he said, "Keep your eyes peeled. We might see some of those yearlings anytime now." Just then we got to where we could see over into a wide valley and saw a big bunch of these yearlings. They took off at once for the timber. He yelled, "Head them Hall. Don't let them get in that timber." We both put spurs to our horses and away we went. We had a wild ride for a long time. Finally we had gathered all that were in that bunch and had them headed down a narrow canyon toward a large meadow down in the valley, when suddenly he asked, "Where is that packhorse?"

I said, "I don't know. The last time I saw him a fellow by the name of Adams was leading him."

"Oh hell, he's halfway back to the ranch by now." When he had seen those yearlings he dropped the lead rope and the pony was waiting for just such a chance to take off back home.

After some pretty strong language, he said, "All right, Hall, this is it. You just take his trail and follow him on back to the ranch."

I said, "What are you going to do?"

He said, "I'm going on. I have to get as many as I can of these doggies."

I said, "Well then, let's ride."

He said, "No, I wouldn't ask you to do this. You have had nothing to eat since early this morning and there's no chance to get anything until tomorrow night. It would take a REAL man to stand that."

It was my turn to say, "Oh hell, let's ride."

Just about dark, after we had gotten the yearlings that we had gathered into a fenced meadow (and we had gathered quite a bunch of them), we came to a little cabin that was used as a side camp. There was a shed and a small corral for the horses and we found some hay for them but no grain. We went to the cabin and built a good fire in the fireplace, and there we sat through the hours of a long night, mostly just staring into the fire. There was not much conversation. I should have done more talking but I was determined not to force any conversation. I never wanted a cup of coffee more in my life, but I didn't complain about it. He would stir occasionally and cuss the packhorse.

Before daylight we were mounted and out to find more yearlings. It had cleared and the sun shone bright and warm. By sundown we had made almost a complete gather. We couldn't get a count on them but he said he believed we had most of them, if not all. It turned out later we had all but five head.

He felt very happy about it, and said, "You know over the ridge there's a camp the Epersons have and they always keep extra horses there. Let's go over and see if we can find fresh horses."

So we rode over and sure enough there were several saddle horses in the meadow. He said, "We might find something to eat in the cabin," so we searched but nothing was to be found.

There was a telephone between this camp and the Adams ranch, operated on the barbed wire fence. He said, "I'll try it and see if I can get through to Edna." After much cranking he got through to his wife. I heard him ask her if the packhorse had come in, and from what he said I knew the horse was home. He told her how very pleased he was to gather the yearlings. The way he yelled over that phone, I think she could have heard him if she had stepped outside. He told her he had the best cowboy help he had ever had, and how he could not have made the gather without it. Then he said, "Edna, cook up every darn thing on the ranch. We have fresh horses and should be home in a coupla hours." I could say "Amen" to that about the cooking.

We went out and got on the fresh horses, and I thought we would hit a high lope for the ranch. It was one of the most beautiful moonlight nights I think I ever saw; a full moon shone almost as bright as day and thousands of diamonds were shining in the snow.

He turned in his saddle and looked at me a long time. Then he said, "All right, cowboy, I've been a damned fool and you have been wonderful. I'll never be able to put in words what I feel down here deep inside. I can never pay you for what you have done. I won't try, but I do want to talk to you. For years I have had something bottled up down deep inside me. I have been miserable and made life miserable for my family and all about me. I have held resentment, been bitter and harsh. I guess Edna and I have been about as happy as most couples but there has always been something lacking in our marriage and lately it has gotten worse."

He paused, and said, "I have done more serious thinking the past two days than ever before in my life. My life seems so empty. I am wondering if what has been lacking in my life and in our home might not be religion. I have always thought that religion was for women and weak-minded people. A preacher tried for a long time to convert me and he rubbed me the wrong way so bad that I developed a real hate for all preachers. Now I know I am wrong. I want you to tell me what religion means to you, what it can mean to a real man such as you have proved to be."

As we rode down that cold mountain trail that night I tried to tell Frank Adams what my religion meant to me and what I knew it could mean to him and to his home. When we got to the home corral he reached over and gave me his hand, and said, "That's for me."

We unsaddled and walked up to the house. His wife was at the door to welcome us. He took her in his arms and crushed her to him until she said, "Oh Frank, are you really that glad to see me?"

"I was never more glad to see you than right now," he said. "I have something very special to tell you after supper. But now, let's eat." We sat down at the table to such a feast as I have seldom seen. It really seemed she had cooked as he had told her — everything on the ranch.

When we had literally gorged ourselves, he said, "Now let's just leave everything like it is here on the table and go in and sit before the fire and talk. We'll wash the dishes and clean up later, won't we, cowboy?" (Now he was calling me cowboy.)

When he had put a fresh log on the fire, he turned to me and said, "Now I want you to tell Edna and Ella May [the daughter] what you told me coming down the trail tonight." Turning to Edna he said, "I told Ralph [now it was Ralph] what a miserable fool I have been, how my life and our home had suffered, and I asked him to tell me what religion could mean to all of us. Now I want him to tell you what he told me."

After we had talked a long time and they had asked many questions, I picked up a Bible from the table and read to them and said, "Let us kneel down and say a prayer together." After I had prayed, I said, "Frank, don't you want to say your own prayer?" I think of all the prayers I have heard uttered, the most wonderful prayer I have ever heard came from that old cowboy's heart and lips as he poured out his very soul to his God out in that ranch home that cold night.

He got up off his knees and threw his arms around his wife and said, "Edna, I will be a Christian husband and father as you have always wanted me to be."

Then Ella May came over and threw her arms around the two of them as they clung together and said, "Me, too, Daddy."

And I said, "Yes, and you, too, Ella May."

In Times of Need

1916

IT SEEMS TO ME that of all the loneliness and the yearning of the Christian heart, the one that goes deepest and causes the most suffering is to be cut off from the privileges of Christian worship and Christian fellowship. The yearning to hear the Gospel message preached is widespread, especially in times of sorrow and great need.

During the time of the developing and settling of this western area, the Sunday School missionary found many of these lonely Christian people; always there was the urge to go to them with the Gospel message of hope and comfort.

One experience early in my ministry will live with me always. I had promised to work through a big roundup and had two days before we were to start gathering the cattle. I had heard of a tiny community of homesteaders in a big basin of the rugged mountains along the New Mexico-Arizona border and decided I would visit them.

Upon arriving I found a one-room schoolhouse, with one teacher and about a dozen pupils. The teacher greeted me cordially and told me how glad the people would be to know that a minister was in the community and would be so glad if I would have a preaching service in the little schoolhouse that night.

"If you can stay and preach for us," she said, "I'll dismiss the school a little early so the children can get the word to everyone in the community." And, she added, "There are two families who live way down in the south end of the basin who would love to come if they knew about it. They have no children in school, and I have no way to get word to them. Perhaps you could drive and tell them."

I assured her I would be happy to do so.

By the time the hour arrived for the service the schoolhouse was packed. Several of the folks had brought along their oil lanterns to light the room. I brought in from my car a little folding organ and asked if anyone would play it for the service. There was a long silence. Then one lady spoke up, "Mrs. Blake will, I am sure."

But Mrs. Blake protested that she could not play the organ.

The lady insisted, "Oh yes, you can. You told us you used to play for your Sunday School."

"That has been so long," exclaimed the other lady. "I haven't touched one for twenty years."

I went over to Mrs. Blake and urged her, and reluctantly she consented. A box was found for a stool. When she sat down and started to put her fingers on the keyboards, I noticed her hands were shaking, but when she began to play an old familiar hymn they were steady and sure. How we all did enjoy the little organ and singing together.

Somehow — I don't know why — I had a feeling that there was something very special, very significant, about that service. There seemed to be an unusual feeling of reverence and awe in the hearts of the people. After preaching my sermon I did something I so often do at times and in places where they so seldom have opportunity to hear the Gospel or to make a public profession of their faith. I said, "As we sing our closing hymn if anyone of you would like to

61

accept my Savior as your Savior and go out to live Christian lives, you come and stand here with me."

Five people came forward, two couples and a young girl, perhaps sixteen years of age.

After a special prayer for them, and the benediction, the girl who had made her profession of faith rushed up to me and began to tell me how wonderful it all was. Then she said, "Mr. Hall, you are to spend the night at our home."

I told her I was very sorry but that I had told the cowboys I would be with them early the next morning to start the roundup and I would have to drive back that night to keep my word.

She said, "You mean you can't go? Mr. Hall you don't understand. Mother and Father are home waiting for you. My mother has been so sick for a long time, and has hoped and prayed for a preacher to come before she dies. When I told her you were going to preach she said, 'My prayers have been answered.' I think she has been clinging to life these last few days hoping a preacher would come. I am afraid to go back and tell her you can't."

I asked, "Where do you live?"

"Just a little way up the big canyon, about five miles."

I asked, "Can I drive the car up?"

She said, "I'm sure you can make it. The road is not too bad."

I asked if she would ride with me and show me the way.

"Of course. I'll turn my horse loose and he'll go home."

I won't soon forget that drive up that canyon that dark night. When we were almost to the home a big old oak stump suddenly showed up in the middle of the road. There was no going over or around it so we walked the rest of the way. Her father met us, carrying a lantern and was so glad to see us. He put a friendly arm around my shoulder and told me how much it meant to have me come, how very ill his wife was and how she almost slipped away twice in the past few days.

"She is wonderful," he said, "the best Christian I have ever known. She is so anxiously waiting to see you."

As we walked into the little home the daughter slipped on ahead of us, rushing over to the bedside. She put her arm around her mother and words poured out: "Oh, Mother, I wish you could have been there. I wish you could have heard the little organ and Mr. Hall's sermon. And Mother, I am a Christian. I accepted Christ tonight and stood up before everyone to tell everybody that I am a Christian, like you and Dad wanted me to be."

I saw the mother cling to her saying, "I'm so happy, I'm so glad," and then, "Did he come?"

The daughter said, "Oh, I'm so sorry. I forgot. Yes, Mother, here is Mr. Hall."

I took her frail hand and looked into her face that was filled with a glow of peace, serenity beyond description. "Now," she said, "I can go home. My prayers have been answered. Please read out of my Bible."

I did. Then she whispered, "Say a prayer."

A few more words together and I could tell she was very weary. She lay back on her pillow and whispered, "Thank you, good night."

The father and daughter could not find words to express their feeling of gratitude. He said, "If only you could be here when she is gone, you could give her a Christian burial."

I told him where I would be the next few days at the roundup and that if he would get word to me I would come.

Three days later a message came to me that she had passed away, and asking me if I would come. I went, got to the old stump in the road, where they had a wagon waiting so we could take the little organ to the cemetery. What a privilege it was to be with the family in their time of sorrow.

As I drove back to the roundup I knew that if I never had any other experience in my ministry, I would say, "It has been worth it — just to be with these people in their time of need."

Life As a Sunday School Missionary

SOON AFTER WE WERE MARRIED, Lillie Bess became ill and we had to rush her to the hospital in Roswell. After she recovered from surgery the doctor told me not to take her back to Lincoln, New Mexico where we were living at the time. The altitude was too high and he wanted her near a hospital and doctor. We moved our headquarters to Post, Texas where I served the little Presbyterian church as a stated supply (A clergyman who without formal installation supplies a pulpit for a limited time as a congregation's acting pastor.) for a short time. A little later we were asked to serve the little church at Quanna, Texas for a brief term, also as a stated supply. This, like the stay at Post was a happy experience.

In 1919 other health conditions caused us to move again. My younger sister developed tuberculosis of a terminal state. I had been laid low with influenza during the big epidemic in 1918 and had not fully recovered. The doctor suspected tuberculosis and advised me to go somewhere along the eastern slope of the Rockies in Colorado and to continue to live out-of-doors. So we were asked to move headquarters to La Porte, Colorado, where I could serve the little church there by preaching Sunday mornings and evenings, and continue my work with the ranch people over a wide area. There was time to work in the roundups, preaching in ranch homes and in the roundups through the days of the week and on Sunday afternoons. For three years this was indeed a rich and rewarding experience, establishing close friendships that have lasted until this day, blessing and enriching our lives.

In 1923 I was asked to become a Sunday School missionary for Boulder Presbytery, in which capacity I continued for two years. This enabled me to spend more time with the ranch people and cowboys.

In 1925 I was asked to come back to New Mexico to become synodical missionary for the whole state. Soon the synod put in a full-time synod executive and I was released to give my full time to Sunday School missions and continue as a missionary to the ranch people and the cowboys.

The work of Sunday School missions began in 1887 by an act of the General Assembly, establishing a pioneer force to reach out into the fast-developing country, mostly heading west. It had a comparatively short history of seventy-five years and I have had the great privilege of serving nearly half a century with this group of devoted and consecrated men.

The fruits of the ministry of the Sunday School missionary are still being reaped today. As of 1939 more than 2,300 churches had grown out of the little Sunday Schools established by Sunday School missionaries.

In 1940 I was asked to serve as the supervisor of all our Sunday School missionary work west of the Mississippi River, which gave me an opportunity to extend my work among ranch people.

It is time for me to introduce my co-worker through the years, Roger B. Sherman; a very close pal for more than half a century.

Roger served through World War I and was a good

soldier. After the war he came to New Mexico and filed on a homestead.

We really began working together when he came to help us construct the Sandia conference grounds. We would work together during the week and I would go out to some mission point for the weekend. He usually would go with me and it was during this time I learned of his burning heart and his desire to become a Sunday School missionary.

I asked Mr. Somerndike, the director of the Department of Sunday School Missions, with headquarters in New York, to allow me to take Roger on as a lay missionary and put him in a very needy field in Nevada. He agreed. I got Roger a used Ford car and told him I would go with him to Nevada and spend a few days with him, getting him started on the new field. We took our bedrolls and camp outfit and drove to Nevada. It was a time of rich fellowship.

I won't ever forget our last camp together before I started for home. We had a season of prayer together, each of us rededicating our lives to the work we loved. We camped a few miles out of town, as I had to catch an early train for home. He drove me to the railroad station where I checked my bedroll, said good-bye, got on the train and walked back to the rear platform. As the train pulled out, the sun was just coming up over the eastern horizon. Roger stood there in the middle of the railroad tracks, waving his old hat. When the train turned around a bend and I could not see him anymore, it gave me a lonesome feeling for him.

I bowed my head and prayed that it might be the beginning of a great ministry for him. It proved to be true, for he has indeed had a rich and blessed ministry.

I soon had a desperate need for him in New Mexico and asked for permission to bring him back. It was granted, and what a great help he was to me. When I had an especially hard job to do such as building a small chapel on a field, I would ask Roger to come help. He always was a top hand, no matter what we were doing, and always carried the heavy end of the load. Together we constructed

66

a number of chapels out across the synod, with the help of men in the local communities.

I had started the youth camp conference and couldn't have done without him. He drove one of the two trucks needed to move our gear, and helped put up all the tents and run the camps for up to a hundred young people.

We traveled from the Mexican border almost to the Canadian border; for about twenty-five years we would leave the last of May and get home about Labor Day. On thousands of nights we have unrolled our bedrolls lying side by side, out under the stars. The story of my life could also be the story of his life, for together we have lived and worked. My life has been enriched and blessed beyond measure by his companionship and Christian love.

Always I had trouble if I wanted to move Roger and his wonderful wife, Bessie, to another field. No one wanted to see them go. In one place a cowboy said, "You just can't do this. The people think Roger hung the moon and Bessie told him how."

After a few years of service and study in Pecos Valley Presbytery, Roger was ordained a minister of the Gospel.

Living Outdoors

I HAVE LIVED IN CAMP most of my life. Except when I was at home, I don't think I stayed inside overnight for about twenty-five years.

Almost always when I had a service in a community someone would insist that I go with them for the night. But there are two reasons why I have camped. First, if you are constantly on the road through the winter, you may stay one night in a home where the people are more fortunate than others, where you have your own bed and sometimes a room to yourself, the room heated and supplied with plenty of warm, clean blankets. The next night you are with a family less fortunate and you may be asked to sleep in the bed with one or two of the boys, and sometimes you find a lot more company in that bed as well.

You know what I mean. The old dog always wants to sleep either on the bed or under it to scratch fleas all night. Or maybe you will be in the back room where no one has slept all winter, with no heat and not enough cover. The coldest thing I know of is a bed where the sheets are so cold they feel wet. Sometimes the snow blows through the cracks and you don't get warm all night.

You often find by changing beds every night that you

soon have the sniffles and a cold develops and you have to cut your trip short and go home to take care of it.

I have a good warm bed and know how to fix it. I can always sleep warm even in zero weather or far below — I have often shaken a foot of snow off my tarp in the morning. When it gets bitter cold out in the high country, it is usually very still. You build a good fire and put your bedroll close to it but not too close. You undress, put on your pajamas, and toast your toes by the fire until your feet are good and warm, and crawl in. I can truthfully say I have never suffered from cold in my bedroll. I have never caught a cold while sleeping out all winter, and I have never carried a tent nor gone in a house on account of a storm.

The other reason you need to camp is that the people will kill you with kindness and by feeding you too much. They don't have the opportunity to visit very often and will keep you up until the wee hours of the morning talking and visiting. I have been to homes where they had a list of questions, saved up maybe for a year.

When they get down that written list, I know I am in for it. They can go to bed the next night at dark, but you are passed along to someone else who is just as anxious to visit and the nights get pretty short.

What I do is to go to the homes, visit until a decent bedtime, then get in the car and drive a few miles and camp.

It is quite an occasion when the preacher comes to visit. Folks seem to think all preachers are big eaters, and I guess they are right. They put the big pot on and cook everything they have in the house that is good to eat. If you don't eat as much as that old fellow does who has been out working hard all day — and who has not had a meal like that since the preacher was there last year — they think you are finicky or don't like the food.

Now I can eat as much as any of them, and enjoy it. The only trouble is that next day. The host can fast but the missionary is pushed on to the next family where the fare is the same, or sometimes not so good and very greasy.

69

Well, pretty soon, if you do this every day, your stomach rebels and you have to lay off.

I eat often with folks, but only about once a day. In camp I can cook what I should eat and no more.

It is just better to stay in camp.

I remember one night when Roger and I were invited into a homesteader's where they were having a very difficult time and had little furniture and little to eat. We agreed to eat supper with them but we felt we were taking the food out of the mouths of the children. Roger was sitting across the table from me on a nail keg. We were eating out of tin plates, with these old three-prong forks. I had it on Roge because I had a fork with three prongs still intact, though a little bent. Roge had one with only two prongs left on it. I had a lot of fun watching him chase peas on that tin plate with that old two-prong fork. He caught a few.

During the summer when we were busy with youth camps and camp meetings, we often had to drive long hours at night over bad mountain roads. I remember one night when we were driving on the Continental Divide where there were many hills, steep grades, and very sharp curves. I was driving a new two-ton Dodge truck, with the cab over the motor. I was mighty proud of it.

It was pouring down rain and visibility was almost nil. All of a sudden the arm on the throttle of the carburetor got turned over so that when I stepped on the gas the motor slowed up. If I pushed it to the floor, the motor would idle. If I let up on it going downhill, the motor would race, speeding up to about seventy miles an hour. We didn't dare stop, for fear that the narrow mountain road and in that storm someone might run into us.

We would start down a steep grade and around a sharp curve, I would forget and let up on the throttle to slow down and instead would shoot ahead. The seminary student riding with me knew for sure we were going to go right over

70

the side of the mountain and down into that deep canyon a thousand feet. I wasn't so sure about it myself.

We finally found a place where we could get off the side of the road. The student said, "Thank goodness." We got our flashlights and a screwdriver and got down under the truck to see if we could fix it. But with the cab over the engine, I couldn't get to the carburetor. We decided to drive on another seventy-five miles, as we were running behind time and did not dare stop for the night. It was a wild ride. Next morning we were able to get the truck fixed and rode on safely, but I was not quite so proud of it anymore.

One summer night when Tom Meyers and I were at the Apache Creek conference grounds to get the camp set up, a skunk came prowling into the kitchen as we sat by the fire talking. He found some kitchen scraps we had thrown out after supper. We knew then he wouldn't leave.

We didn't want to disturb him; we knew if we alarmed him he would ruin the camp for the next day when the young people arrived. Yet we knew we had to get rid of him or the boys would chuck him and the whole camp would be ruined. The question was, how? He was very bold, and didn't seem to mind us at all; he would even pass under our chairs.

I offered Tom a good sum of money if he would grab the critter by the tail and take him out of the camp. I assured him that if he would grab him by the tail when it was up and jerk him off the ground, the skunk could do nothing. (I had heard this was so but had never seen it tried.)

Tom said, "Nothing doing."

It happened later that Tom was sitting there leaning back in his chair when the skunk came close enough to me for me to grab his tail, which was sticking straight up. As I grabbed the animal and jerked him in the air, Tom went

71

over backwards in his chair and lit out. I carried the skunk out of camp. Tom came with a club and tapped him over the head. That was the end of the skunk, and no damage done. No scent of him was left in camp.

I have enjoyed having many college or seminary students come and work with us in the camps and conferences through the summer. They seemed to enjoy it even though we worked them pretty hard.

I remember when one young fellow named Eddie came. I took him off the train and headed for the high country. It was Saturday afternoon and we drove late to get within driving distance of the place where I was to preach on Sunday.

We were up early the next morning and on the way. After Sunday School I preached a long sermon. Some folks who lived ten miles away insisted that we go to their place for lunch. We went. The lady had to churn after we got home, to have butter for lunch, so it was late before we got to eat. I knew Eddie was about to cave in, as it had been a long time since breakfast. At last we sat down and dishes began passing around. Eddie had his plate well filled when the big bowl of freshly churned butter came by. He had never seen freshly churned butter before, and thought it was gravy. He had some mashed potatoes on his plate so he remarked that he sure liked good gravy. Nobody said anything while he poured it on by the spoonsful. He had a lot of trouble cleaning his plate that day.

All of our children have gone with me to help in the camps almost from the time they could crawl. As they grew older they took part in the program — teaching classes, conducting vespers, helping with the cooking, pot washing, and anything else.

I don't know how I could have gotten along without them. Any one of them could cook a meal for a hundred or however many there were to feed. During the war years our daughter, Betty, really made a hand. We were short-

72

handed and she drove a truck all summer and did some of everything.

Once we had been out for nearly a hundred nights in our bedrolls and living in camp. When we finally got home in the middle of a hot afternoon, Betty rushed into the kitchen to greet her mother and get a drink of water. She drank a glass and a half.

Busy talking to her mother she just tossed the half-glass that was left on the kitchen floor, as she would have done in camp. I almost didn't get to take her along the next summer.

Camping in a Bad Snowstorm

I NEVER GO OUT ON A TRIP WITHOUT my bedroll and sometimes I've been mighty glad to have it along.

While driving from Cheyenne to Gillette, Wyoming one winter day, I stopped in Casper to get gas and visit an old friend who owned the gas station and motel. We had a good visit for a short time. I knew I had to keep moving to reach Gillette that night, as I had a very important meeting at 8:00 A.M. the next day.

When I was ready to say good-bye he said, "You're not going anywhere, you're going to spend the night with us. We have a room for you here in the motel." He insisted that it would not be safe to make the drive that night. "Everything is just right for a ground blizzard," he said. "It was a beautiful, warm day, no wind, no clouds, two years ago when we had the worst blizzard I ever saw. In that storm I lost 2,500 head of sheep. You are not going."

He walked over, took the keys out of my car, and stuck them in his pocket. It was just at sunset. "Supper is ready. Come on and we'll eat, then we can have a good visit and you can go on in the morning."

I had a most difficult time convincing him that I had

eaten my supper at a little cafe down the street and that I really had to move on. Very reluctantly he gave me my keys, and I started on my way.

There were about twelve inches of snow on the ground but the roads were clear, and I anticipated no trouble. It was a beautiful night with the stars shining brightly. I was listening to the car radio as I drove when the program was interrupted; the anouncer said a severe ground blizzard was coming in, and urgently he warned everyone to get off the highways, seek shelter, and protect the livestock. Then every five minutes he kept repeating the warning.

I stopped my car, got out and looked around. It was still clear and beautiful. I was more than halfway to Gillette and knew that I could make it in about an hour's drive. I got back in the car and speeded up, driving as fast as I dared. As I topped out over a small hill I could see the lights at Gillette just a few miles away, so I relaxed and thought everything was okay.

There was a small arroyo that I had to cross, with a steep hill just beyond. The road was narrow and curved around the side of the hill with a deep canyon on one side. I was almost to the top when all of a sudden I hit the blizzard.

High wind with blowing snow made visibility absolutely nil; I might as well have been blindfolded with black velvet. I stopped the car and got out but could not see a thing. I was afraid to stay there for fear another car might run into me. I got the flashlight but it didn't help much. I walked about ten steps along the edge of the road and saw that my wheels were headed right for a few feet, so I got in and drove, then repeated the performance until I could get safely off the road and into the ditch. I thought I would wait a little while and maybe it would let up a bit after the first fury of the storm.

It had become terribly cold all at once, so I turned on my heater in the car, but soon discovered it was getting worse instead of better. I decided the best thing I could do was to get into my bedroll.

I put the bedroll right beside the car for a little shelter as I got into bed. Sometime before a cowboy had given me a heavy bearskin overcoat. He was a very large man and that old coat was too heavy to wear, but I always took it along. I put it on top of my blanket and under the tarp that was the cover for my entire bed. Then I put the shovel close-by so I could dig out my bed and the car after the storm, and I crawled into the bedroll.

I think that old coat weighed about forty pounds — at least it felt that way on top of me — but it felt mighty good. I had a nap, then woke up weighted down with snow that drifted over the car and on top of me. I had to crawl out and pull my bedroll out in the open where the snow would not drift over me so, and finished a good night's sleep.

When morning came the stormy wind was still blowing. I could see only about six inches of the top of the car, so I decided the best place for me was to stay in the bedroll where I was warm.

About noon the blizzard began to blow itself out. I got up and shoveled my way to the car, then shoveled my bedroll out.

I was beside a barbed wire fence. The fence posts had not been cut off at the top wire, some of them sticking up two feet above the fence. I had a sharp axe and cut off the top of the post for firewood, without damaging the fence. By drawing some gas out of the car I got a good fire going in a spot I had cleared of snow. There was plenty of food in my chuck box so I had a wonderful breakfast and plenty of good hot coffee.

I shoveled the snow away from the car and a path to the road. Much to my surprise the car started all right, but the snow was too deep to travel. Just about sundown I could hear a bulldozer coming my way, clearing the road. When it arrived the fellows pulled me on the road and I could go on to Gillette.

I found it had been thirty-seven degrees below zero. Three people had frozen to death within ten miles of me. Thanks to my bedroll, I had been safe and warm.

A Change Of Leaders

DURING THE LIFE OF THE DEPARTMENT of Sunday School Missions, I had the privilege of working under the leadership of three great men who were the directors of our department: First, Mr. J. M. Somerndike who served for forty-four years; then Dr. Everett B. King; and later the Reverend J. Earl Jackman.

The following is a short speech I made at the time Everett King retired as our director to become pastor of First Presbyterian Church in Albuquerque, New Mexico, and Earl Jackman came to take his place.

Thank you, Everett.

It is always good for us to come together in this fine fellowship. As we do, certain great spirits seem to hover near. All but four of us here in this room served under the leadership of our beloved and honored Mr. Somerndike. His presence and spirit ever seem to be with us. We have not forgotten him. There is today and ever will be a sacred place in our hearts and memories for this noble and beloved man.

When God called him home so suddenly, a great sense of loss and loneliness engulfed us. We were cast down and

78

prayed earnestly that God would give us another to lead who possessed the same vision and purpose. Our prayers were answered. He gave us one, not to take Mr. Somerndike's place in our hearts, as he had no desire to do; rather, our hearts were opened to him and he just walked right in and made a great place for himself.

Everett, you have no idea how large that place is. You were a great leader and friend, day by day leading us nearer to the great, loving heart of our God. You were ever a great inspiration, constantly challenging us to a more devoted and consecrated service. We placed many problems on your broad shoulders, and many burdens on your great Christian heart. There was always the feeling that you cared, and you so constantly shared.

Now with all our hearts we say thank you; thank you for every prayer you prayed with and for us, for your constant desire and effort to build up a real spiritual power in the life of each one of us that might render a more complete and fuller service to our Lord and the cause we love so much. Everett, we thank God for you and wish to assure you that you will ever have a great place of honor and love in our hearts. We love you still.

When Everett was called by the Lord into another field of service, we felt a great sense of loss, and once more we were cast down; we again besought the great Eternal God to give another with the same zeal, passion and vision. We feel our prayers have been answered again as Earl Jackman has been brought to us.

Mr. Jackman, you can never take the place in our hearts of either of these men, but our hearts are open to you and we say, "Come in." You make and hold your own place. We pledge our loyalty and prayers. Lead on; we are ready to follow.

Everett, present to us your friend and our new chief.

The Bachelor and the Ladies

IN ONE OF THE SMALL COW TOWNS where they had developed a high school, the superintendent of the schools suddenly began to disappear over the weekends. He was a bachelor and the lady teachers were very curious about where he went for those weekends. They suspected that he had a lady friend somewhere, and they told me to watch for him as I traveled over the field, and to try to find out where he went and why.

A few weeks later I rode into a small town about a hundred miles from where the curious teachers lived. I got in late and went to the boardinghouse where two other lady teachers stayed. One of them was an old friend, as we grew up in the same community. She was full of the dickens.

When I arrived at the boardinghouse on a Saturday night, I found everyone was just finishing supper so I ate alone at the big table. The two teachers sat with me at the table to talk. I took my dishes back to the kitchen and visited for a minute with the cook.

When I came back to the dining room these two teachers were in a huddle over in one corner, giggling and almost in hysterics. They asked if I wanted to see the funniest thing I had ever seen in my life. I tried to tell them I wasn't interested, but they kept on until they got me over by the heavy curtain that hung in the opening between the dining room and the parlor. Then they whispered, "Get down on the floor and peep under the curtain." They fairly pushed me to the floor and I peeped in under the curtain.

It was really an amusing sight. There was the missing school superintendent and a most attractive lady, sitting in straight chairs about two feet apart, each of them reaching out and holding hands.

The heavy curtain was divided in the center. Suddenly each one of those crazy ladies pulled back her side of the curtain and there I was lying on the floor looking up into the face of the superintendent — a man I knew very well.

I just crawled under the table that, lucky for me, was very near.

I wrote him a note of apology later and I never did give the curious teachers the satisfaction of knowing I had found where the superintendent went on weekends.

81

A Speech To Co-Workers

AT OUR ANNUAL conference of Sunday School missionaries in Denver, Colorado in 1937 we celebrated our fiftieth anniversary. We had nearly a hundred missionaries present.

FOR DENVER — OUR TASK TODAY

Mr. Somerndike and fellow workers:

For a little while we have been walking back through the years to the Voice of the past. As we have walked along memory's road with Mr. Somerndike our hearts have been thrilled with the wonderful stories of triumph of the Gospel through the past fifty years, blessed years filled with glorious achievement.

It was a great day for our church back yonder fifty years ago when the General Assembly of 1887 gave to that new agency its charter and sent out the Sunday School missionaries with the great commission to go out and minister to the spiritually neglected youth of our country. We have rejoiced as we have listened to the voice of the past. Now let us tune our ears to the voice of the hour and the call of tomorrow. I am sure I speak the sentiment of each of

82

you, my fellow workers, when I say that we feel very humble as the mantle of the heroes falls upon our shoulders.

We lift up our eyes and look upon the field white unto the harvest. We behold upwards of seventeen million boys and girls, or about half of the youth of America of school age, without any kind of religious training. We see also the hundreds and thousands of young people in our little mission Sunday Schools whose hands must be placed in the hand of God, and whose young lives must be trained for Christian service. We see, also, the vast unchurched areas, the land that must be possessed for Christ and His Kingdom. Throughout our various fields we see the lonely and isolated homes and hear the cry of those hungry hearts and souls for the Gospel message of comfort and hope, and the many who need the message of salvation.

We are out under the same charter and with the same great commission. Through the years we have lost nothing of the original program, but rather it has been broadened and enlarged to embrace a systematic program of Christian education: keeping apace and utilizing the latest and most modern methods of Christian training. We have a very definite choice of missionary service that is worthy to challenge and enlist the finest men of our church in our ranks. I shall not go into the details of that program at this time for I am sure it will be covered in all details in this conference. The task is as great and presents a challenge as great as at any time in the history of our church.

What is our task today? We are sent to the neglected people of America, especially the youth, to preach, to train. It is ours to become the pastor of the pastorless, to visit the isolated homes, to establish family religion.

For our work we have a very fine program outlined for us to follow, but in some times and in some instances I fear we have allowed the program to become the end toward which we are striving rather than a means toward the end. In other words, we have become so absorbed in putting on and carrying out the program we have forgotten the *one thing* the program is to help us to accomplish.

One of the greatest tasks we face today is that of training and developing leadership. This is not easy but I think that it is one of the weak links in most of our work. In so many communities the whole responsibility rests on one or two people. We allow the work to be built about a personality. In so many communities if you take out one or two people the Sunday School will die. I am sure this will be discussed later in the program.

For the past few years Christian work has been very difficult in so many ways and in so many places. We have all met so many discouraged people who have felt whipped, licked — who seemed to be fighting with their backs to the wall. Over and over again we hear them say, "We just must keep the Sunday School open. We will not let it die." Thank God for them. We have all been on the defensive. We have been willing to defend with our very lives. But it seems to me as we face our task today that we must no longer be satisfied to defend, but that we must go out to *proclaim*. Oh, if we could only rally our forces of righteousness and launch out in a great offensive movement, unfurling the banner of our Lord to the breeze and holding it high, going out to conquer in His name.

I wonder what would happen if each one of us here would go back to our fields from this conference and call a mass meeting in each one of our communities in which we serve, and with our own hearts on fire with zeal and passion call upon the people to leave the wall they have been pushed back against, and with rededicated lives go out to put on a great spiritual campaign for our Lord.

We hear it said very often these days that God and the church are being tested and that in this modern day they have failed. When I hear this it makes my blood run cold. Instead of the great Eternal God and His church being tested, we of this day are being weighed in the balance and I feel sure we are being found wanting.

As we face the great task before us, I think there are some grave dangers that face us as individuals: There is the great danger of losing our vision and "Where there is no Vision the people perish." This is also true of the missionary. If we as individuals lose our vision, we are doomed to certain failure.

There is also danger lest we lose our zeal and allow the altar fires to burn low in our own hearts. I know all of us have our dark and discouraging days and often we seem to meet with defeat on every hand. We are prone to feel that "We alone are left." We need constantly to renew the fires in our own hearts and lives from the altar fire of His great love and sacrifice. If we are to meet the needs of our day and perform our tasks as Sunday School missionaries, we must remember always that we are *missionaries* and never allow ourselves to think of our work as a mere job, but remembering always that we are the witnesses of our Lord and often the only representative He has in large areas.

If we are to measure up to our task today we must cultivate loyalty; loyalty to our Lord, loyalty to our church, loyalty to our Board of National Missions, loyalty to our fields of service and loyalty to our fellow workers. We must stand together as a unit, for there is a peculiar tie that binds us together. Our lives must be dedicated to the great cause of Sunday School missions.

I can think of no more pathetic human being than a missionary who has lost his vision and allowed the fires of zeal and passion to go out in his own heart and life. For if he does, he will become bitter, hard, harsh, and sour. He will then settle down to travel in a rut and be satisfied to just get by, just exist.

God forbid that any one of our group should ever lose his vision and zeal, but with hearts that are constantly mellowed by His great love and sacrifice and with the flame of passion and zeal burning in our souls, may we go out to conquer in His name.

The Sunday School At Solo

1928

A REPORT FROM *our Sunday School missionary, the Reverend Ralph J. Hall, Synodical Missionary, Albuquerque, New Mexico.*
To the Members of the Collingwood Avenue Presbyterian Sunday School, Toledo, Ohio.

My Dear Friends:

As I have been assigned to you by the Department of Sabbath School Missions of our board, as your missionary I want to know you, and I want you to know me.

First of all I want to tell you that I am happy to have the privilege of representing you out here on this great mission field in the interest of our Lord's kingdom. It helps greatly when the task is hard, and you are somewhat discouraged, to know that there is someone vitally interested in you, and backing you up; so it will be mine oftentimes to remember that you are backing me, and helping with your prayers and means.

This is truly a great mission field; I think it is the greatest in all of our church, here at home. New Mexico is a large state, covering more than 122,000 square miles. It is sparsely settled and oftentimes the distances are great and the people are far between.

It requires a great deal of travel to cover it. My average mileage in doing my work is about 2,000 miles per month. Last year for the twelve months I averaged preaching six times every week, visited in more than a thousand homes, and preached in about a hundred different places — sometimes, not often, in a stately church building, but more often in a little adobe schoolhouse tucked away somewhere by the side of the road, or in the humble home of some homesteader, or in the plaza of some village, or out around the campfire of the cowboys, and many times out on the great Navaho Indian reservations, to the Indians.

The work of National Missions is very interesting in this state because of the variety. We have the work among the Indians, in both reservations and pueblos, and among the Spanish-speaking people. Then there is the work among miners, lumberjacks, and other people living out on the frontier.

I am camped tonight out here near a little place called Ojo Caliente, about a hundred miles from anywhere. I wish that each of you could have been with me today in our Sabbath's worship and work. I preached in a little schoolhouse called Solo. It is only twelve feet wide and twenty feet long, and has one window. It is made of logs and plastered on the inside with mud. I didn't preach in it, for it would not hold the people; so we went outside and built a large fire. The people gathered around it and we had the service. It was the first religious service ever conducted within twenty-five miles of this place.

People were there from twenty-five miles around, bringing their dinners, and coming in lumber wagons, buggies, on horseback, and in Fords.

At ten o'clock I preached for them and then we organized a Sunday School that started off with about forty pupils.

A good many people in it had never been in a Sunday School before.

At noon we all spread our lunch together and at 2:00 P.M. I preached again. Then in the evening we ate what we had left from dinner and had another service. It has been a day that these people will long remember.

I stood at the door of the little schoolhouse and watched the last wagon disappear over the hill, making its way down to a humble home nestling in the canyon below. With their hearty "good-bye" and "come back soon" ringing in my ears, I could not keep back the tears from my eyes because I knew what they were going back to, and they had said, "We will be waiting and praying for you to return soon."

I then got in my car and drove out here in the canyon where I am writing this letter by the light of my campfire. And tonight I will unroll my blankets under the stars and sleep; and as I do so I thank our Heavenly Father for the Holy day with its Sabbath blessings and privileges, and for the opportunity to preach to these folks.

Many of them had not heard a sermon in years; two said to me that for more than forty years they had not heard a sermon. Women who had not heard a sermon since their girlhood days came to me with tears in their eyes and said, "Thank God for your coming; it has been such a wonderful privilege." I just thank God for a place to work in a mission field like this.

And so I could go on telling you of such incidents and of the great mission field out here, but I must stop; my campfire is about out and I have a long, hard drive tomorrow to get to Tierra Amarilla, where I am to preach. I expect to get home about the eighteenth of this month for a day, when the call comes for me to make another extensive trip to the border country.

I shall be very glad to hear from any one of you at anytime. It does me good to hear from friends who are interested and helping in the great work. Any personal letters received will be greatly appreciated. I love the work with all my heart and life, but sometimes it is hard to go on when I have to be away from home all the time. I have a wife and three small children and it is hard to be away from them. I have not had more than a dozen days with them since last April.

May our Heavenly Father richly bless you is my prayer. I am, sincerely your missionary,

Ralph J. Hall
Box 640
Albuquerque, N.M.

A Sunday School Missionary's Dream That Came True

NEVER SHALL I FORGET the cold and bleak winter days of December, 1926, when I followed a dim trail for 120 miles out into an unknown country. The winding trail led me across a desert and a mesa and over the mountains into the new homestead community of Lindrith, New Mexico. This community was more than a hundred miles from the railroad or from any other church, save for a little Spanish church thirty miles away at Cuba. It was many miles away from a telephone, and the nearest medical service was 125 miles away at Albuquerque.

There I found a group of hardy pioneers — 5,000 or more homesteaders who had left homes and friends in Texas and Oklahoma and pushed west to establish new homes. They had settled in this high, cold country with invincible determination to conquer an empire, to establish homes, to organize churches, and to create schools.

I went searching for this group of people in answer to the call of a Christian mother, pleading for religious services for her family and her neighbors.

Never have I received a more cordial welcome in all

my experience as a missionary. They welcomed me by saying, "We have been praying for you to come." Shortly after my arrival messengers were traveling in every direction spreading the good news to the lonely homestead shacks, to the ranches scattered here and there over the hills, and to the logging camps far back in the timber. These messengers went with the word, "The preacher is here. Services tonight in the schoolhouse!"

When darkness settled over the hills, the wind began blowing a gale, sweeping down from the high mountains and bringing with it fine, powdered snow. It was bitter cold. My heart sank within me, for I felt the people would not be able to come, and I knew they were counting on this first religious service. But when the announced hour struck, the people began to arrive at the little half-finished schoolhouse. They came in lumber wagons, in old worn cars, on foot, and on horseback.

A roaring fire was built in an old iron barrel that had been transformed into a stove by cutting a door in the end and making an opening for the stovepipe. Two lighted kerosene lamps vainly tried to push back the deep shadows within the room. A few rough homemade benches were drawn close to the stove, and these benches were filled with women clasping babies to their breasts. The men stood, or squatted on their heels around the walls. The storm that raged outside drove the snow halfway across the dirt floor of the little building, for the cracks between the logs had not been chinked. The folding organ was brought in from my car, and a log was set as a stool for the organist.

The service began. As the first strains of music floated out from the tiny organ a hush fell over the room. How the people did enjoy singing the Gospel songs! They sang out of their hearts. After the reading of the Scripture, I looked into their eager faces and saw many eyes filled with tears — tears of joy because of the privilege of attending this religious service. For some, this was the first time in many long and lonely years.

I felt I wanted to preach the best sermon of my life and my soul was filled with a holy fire when I realized I was to preach the first sermon in this new community. I prayed that night that the service might be the beginning of a great work in the interest of the Kingdom of God.

I dreamed about the organization of a Sunday School, and perhaps a church later. I even dreamed of a church building with a local missionary serving the whole country. It was a heavenly dream. . . .

We had a good service and I think we all felt the power of the Holy Spirit in our midst. At the close of the service my dreams started to come true, for we organized a Sunday School that has never faltered. Through winter's severe cold and summer's intense heat, these people have carried on. During the following three years I visited them as often as I could, helping them with the Sunday School and preaching as many as four sermons in one day.

Soon this group of pioneers began pleading for regular preaching services, for a pastor, for a church organization, for the erection of a church building. I told their story in Philadelphia. God opened the heart of the Carmel Presbyterian Church in Edge Hill, Pennsylvania, to the Macedonian call, and this church pledged to underwrite the salary of a Sunday School missionary. The Reverend J. M. Young answered the call, with his wife and three daughters, and started ministering to these hardy people.

Later I told the story of this work in Minneapolis. The heart of Mr. Nelson Dayton was greatly moved and he and his family provided funds for the church building. How happy the people were that day when, under the leadership of Mr. Young, they went into the forest, cut great pine trees, and dragged the logs to a beautiful hillside where they erected their church with their own hands and without pay. It stands there today the only church building for nearly a hundred miles in any direction — with one exception.

The next step was the erection of a manse, so the men of the community went back into the forest with their axes; they cut logs and dragged them in, building a home for their minister. It stands across the road from the church.

Being true pioneers with high and holy aims of building a Christian community, these people wanted the best for their families. The church had been a source of comfort and strength for them through days of hardship and privation when they had experienced great droughts and bitter cold. They next set about to secure a high school, and again the Sunday School missionary became the captain and led the campaign. Through the State University of New Mexico and the State Board of Education, a high school was assured. So once again these stalwart men marched into the forest, to cut logs for a high school building; once more their prayers were answered and their dreams came true.

The next adventure of these homesteaders was to provide wholesome recreation and Christian fellowship. They leased from the Forest Service six acres of beautiful pine forest on the mountainside, twenty-five miles from the church. There they established a parish conference ground. Under the leadership of the Sunday School missionary they cut a road to the site with their own hands, and there erected a tabernacle for all services in the camp. Over the years they have gathered at this spot for parish meetings, young people's conferences, fifth Sunday meetings, Sunday School institutes, and other assemblies. The camp is one of God's choicest spots. It is a cathedral in itself and has proved to be a great blessing to the whole community.

After organizing the Sunday School, securing a minister, building a church and school, and establishing a conference ground, the people still were faced with the need of medical aid. Many graves had been made in the lonely cemetery on the hill because of the lack of medical care.

The knowledge of untimely deaths, and of the unnecessary suffering of untold numbers who had fought their way through only because of rugged constitutions, weighed heavily on the heart of the Sunday School missionary. Many cold nights he had driven his car over nearly impassable roads to Albuquerque, seeking relief for his suffering people. Finally the climax came. Returning home with a heavy heart from the funeral service for Uncle John Henry, Mr. Young was hailed on the highway by two men. It was ten o'clock at night. The men told their sad story: Leona Brown had died that morning in childbirth. Leona was one of the charter members of the Sunday School. She was a lovely and loyal soul. Her death was a shock to the whole community. Because of the condition of her body, it was impossible to delay funeral arrangements; so near midnight on the lonely hillside under the light of kerosene lanterns, Leona Brown's body was buried in a pine box. Out of his great love for his people, Morton Young said that night, "This must never happen again."

So a meeting was called and the people decided to build a health center. They had no money, but were willing to work. Once again the missionary led them as they cut huge trees and hauled them to a spot near the church where three acres of land had been donated. With their own hands they built a beautiful six-room building. Today it is a health center where regular clinics are conducted. And there is a resident registered nurse, Miss Ruth Herron and her helper Miss Lula Ruth Floyd, who are supported by the Unit of Educational and Medical Work of the Board of National Missions. Their services already have proved to be a blessing to these fine pioneer folks.

The latest chapter is still being written. The little missionary church at Lindrith has so prized its precious possessions that its members are trying to share what they have with others. At Pine Grove, where hearts are hungry for the Gospel, another church has been started. The work goes on under the devoted leadership of the Reverend J. M. Young and his family.

As I survey the Lindrith parish with its dozen or more surrounding stations where regular Christian work is being carried on, I feel that my prayers on that cold December night have been answered and that my dream has come true.

94

The Unit of Sunday School Missions
(A report for 1940)

Under the Board of National Missions, the Unit of Sunday School Missions is trying to reach the unreached boys and girls in America for Christ. There is no other denomination that has Sunday School missionaries in a naitonal program. The task is great. There are seventeen million children in our homeland without a Sunday School, receiving no religious training. Here are some telling figures about the work of the church in this field that "is white unto harvest":

110   commissioned Sunday School missionaries are laboring in thirty-two different states.

600   Sunday Schools were organized and revived last year.

3,000   Sunday Schools are now under these Sunday School missionaries, with a total enrollment of 130,000.

3,000,000   religious tracts and periodicals were distributed last year.

12,000   weekday Bible Schools have been established with a weekly enrollment of 350,000 boys and girls.

3,000   souls were won for Christ under these Sunday School missionaries last year, and more than 115,000 families visited.

A Talk to Missionaries

1943

F OR THE LAST FIFTEEN YEARS of my active ministry I had the privilege of being the supervisor of all our Sunday School work west of the Mississippi. As often as I could I got as many Sunday School missionaries as I could together for a retreat. Sometimes this would be five or six of us with bedrolls in a camp for a couple of days, sometimes forty or fifty together for four days in a hotel or at Menaul School, for a conference discussing every phase of our work.

The following is a copy of my opening talk with about forty Sunday School missionaries in one of our conferences in 1940:

To a great many people, "Go ye into all the world" means only going to China, Japan, Africa, or to some distant place across the sea; but to the Sunday School missionary it means going into the most isolated and neglected parts of his field. It means more than going into villages and the thickly settled communities. It means more than following the paved highways. It often means dim and rugged trails over the mountains or across the parched sands of the desert. It means visiting that lonely and isolated home or community, for the Sunday School missionary must ever be primarily a trailblazer, a pioneer in the work of the Kingdom.

I remember as a lad being held spellbound by the fascinating and thrilling stories told in the home of my father or around my grandfather's fireside, by the old pioneers who would stop to visit with us — stories of the settling of the West, of pioneer trail trips and the thrilling experiences of the Indian scouts. How I often wished that I might have lived a generation earlier that I might have been a scout or a trailblazer leading some great wagon train across an unchartered and unexplored country. How I wished that I might be the first settler in some new land. I often indulged in daydreams, planning the kind of home I would build and the kind of foundation I would lay in that new country; how I would have a part in making and molding the community. In my most fantastic dreams and imaginings, I saw myself as an old man with the country about me developed and dotted with comfortable homes and people saying of me, "He was the first settler; he pioneered in this country; he was the first white man to settle in this valley."

I dreamed of how pleased and happy this would make me, but in my wildest dreams I never thought that they would come true or that I would have a more romantic, thrilling and glorious experience of pioneering than the men who told the fascinating stories by my grandfather's fireside.

What missionary's heart has not thrilled as we have followed some dim trail as the first messenger of Christ into a new country? And what missionary's heart has not been made to burn, and what soul has not been filled with the holy fire, as we have stood in the evening time before a group of earnest people by the dim light of the kerosene lamp in a rough log cabin or adobe schoolhouse? And what visions have come crowding into our minds as we have looked into their eager eyes through which we are able to

97

see souls that are starved and hungry for the "Bread of Life!"

Standing thus, as the first messenger of Christ in one of these communities, and seeing the possibilities for a new Sunday School and the training of the young hearts and lives for Christ and His Kingdom, we have dared to hope and pray for the coming of not only the Sunday School, but for a church organization and a temple of worship.

What a glorious privilege to start the first Sunday School! What a privilege to go back from time to time to visit them and to see the Sunday School grow; to train the teachers, to gather the young people for instruction in the things of the Kingdom; to hold a week of special services and see them come forward and accept your Christ as their Christ; then someday to go back and organize the church and spend a few days working with hammer and saw helping them to erect the house of worship.

Then what Sunday School missionary's heart has not been made to rejoice as we have driven out over the mountains or across the prairies or the desert and stopping at some high vantage point and looking back to see the spire lifting heavenward? Of course, it may not be very stately or grand, but we know to these people living in the lonely community it is verily a temple of God.

And, too, our hearts have been filled with joy in after years when we have gone back and heard them say of us, "He was the first minister to visit our community. He organized the first Sunday School and laid the foundation for our present church and work."

In this I feel I have found a far more glorious field in which to pioneer than did the men who guided the wagon trains across the great plains of the West.

A few weeks ago I had the pleasure of having part in the celebration of the 150th anniversary of the First Presbyterian Church of Pittsburgh. I heard Dr. McCartney give the historical sketch of that church. He told of the first missionaries who came across the Allegheny Mountains to preach and sow the seed of the Gospel, how discouraging it sometimes was and how small the beginning. His description of the missionary trips and the visits of these men might well have been a description of the missionary trips of this group of missionaries assembled in this room; and his description of the beginning of the church might well have been the description of the beginning of some of the churches we organized this past year.

What will be the result of our work 150 years from now no one knows but of this we are sure: It behooves us to be earnest and diligent in the sowing of the seed, to hope and pray that God in His all-wise providence will guide and direct us, and from the sowing of the seed that there may be a bountiful harvest in souls for His Kingdom.

No greater honor or privilege is given to a group of our church than that given to the Sunday School missionaries, for upon us falls the responsibility for practically all of the extension work of the church here in America. It is a sacred commission and one we accept in humility and great devotion. It is not our aim or plan that every mission Sunday School shall grow into a church organization. Oftentimes we organize these schools in camps or in communities where there is no hope of their becoming permanent. But this does not mean that we should be less zealous in the sowing of the seed, because we should realize that in places of this kind it may be the only contact these boys and girls will have with the Gospel of our Lord. And so we count it a privilege to minister to them in His name.

The Presbyterian church is a great mission church. She has ever sought to give the Gospel message to all places without regard to color, race or location. Has the time come for us to take down her banner? Shall we say the task is finished? No, the church is looking to us to carry on. We must not fail. Every trail, every dim road crossing our fields, should present a challenge to the Sunday School missionary because it may lead to a soul we might save for Christ, or a home where we might say a prayer, or perhaps to an isolated camp or community where we may be of service.

It seems to me that there are two phases of our work that we sometimes pass over lightly.

First, that our primary task is the extension work. This does not mean we are not to cooperate with the National Missions Committees in caring for the vacant home mission pulpit, and the nurture and care of our national mission churches; nor that we are to neglect the regular organized Sunday School we have going. They need our help and care but if we are not careful, we will find that we are giving all of our time to these phases of the work and find that we are not pushing out into new fields. In doing the important things we may neglect the most important or our primary task.

However, extension means more than opening up new fields. It means putting a new program in many of our mission Sunday Schools that show little sign of growth and of religious zeal and fervor. I think one reason so many of our schools flourish for a short time and then die, and the reason we are called again and again to reorganize them, is that we have failed to give them a real program. However, this will be discussed in a later paper.

Almost any one of us could spend twice as much time as we have in looking after the work we now have going, and in looking after the mission churches of our presbytery. We are oftentimes tempted to spend our time with the larger schools and in the thickly settled communities. These, I feel, should have a greater portion of our time; but we should not forget that isolated family who never hears a sermon or sees a minister. Stop and call on them and say a prayer around the fireside for the blessings and benedictions of their heavenly Father upon the home. Oftentimes we fail to realize just what these visits mean.

Then there are small Sunday Schools, perhaps with only

a half-dozen scholars; but their lives and souls are just as precious as those in the larger schools.

As to the methods we are to pursue in our extension work, I hope they will be brought out in the discussion to follow.

The second thing I feel we should keep in mind is that we are Sunday School missionaries. That is, that our chief mission is to the children and youth of our fields. I think some of us are prone to become very much discouraged when we visit a community and find only a few older people coming out for our services or taking part in the Bible School. Sometimes because of this we feel that it is not worthwhile and allow the school to die for lack of attention. We should ever remember that in the child we have more than just a soul to be saved from hell. We have a soul and a life of Christian service to save.

I have often wished that we might have the biographies of the first Sunday School missionaries printed. What a source of inspiration they would be for us as their mantles fall upon our shoulders. As we look back and see the glorious work they did, it presents a great challenge to us. In the past forty-four years more than eighty-five percent of all the new Presbyterian churches that have been organized have grown out of our mission Sunday Schools, started by Sunday School missionaries; and today ninety-nine percent of all new churches grow out of our mission Sunday Schools.

Realizing that the church of the future depends upon us and our work, shall we not during this conference dedicate our lives anew to the task that is ours? I would like to suggest that we adopt as our slogan for this year, "The Gospel for the Remotest."

It seems to me there has never been a more glorious hour in which to preach the unsearchable riches of the Gospel of our Lord than this hour and this day in which we live. The world and our nation are burdened with a great anxiety. Distress and poverty are on every hand. Our

101

hearts are made to ache as we visit our fields and hear the stories of distress. So often we hear them say, "We are interested and do so much want to come for the Sunday School and preaching, but we have no feed for our horses nor gas for our car, and it is too far for us to walk." The least we can do is to go to them in their homes.

Shall we not go out to canonize our work with prayer, to baptize it with tears if need be, to fill it with heart and glorify it with soul, so that by and by when time shall be no more and we in His presence stand, we shall hear no man, woman, boy or girl from our fields say, "No man cared for my soul."

We do care, and that is the reason we go.

Study in Sunday School Missions
1932

WESTWARD HO" has ever been the watchword of the Sunday School missionary — not necessarily out toward the setting sun but out into the far and lonely places where live those without Gospel privileges. It is to them that the Sunday School missionary feels the urge to go. He has ever been, and still is, a trailblazer, a pioneer in the things of the Kingdom.

We Sunday School missionaries make what we call missionary journeys. The first thing is to plan the trip so we can reach just as many homes, logging camps, mines, and homestead communities as possible. Next, we send out cards telling the people when we are coming. These cards are sent to the most interested person in each community and camp we are to visit, and he will spread the news.

On the day before we leave, the Ford must be serviced, greased, and tires checked, for it will see some rough traveling before we return. Then we pack the car. The shovel must be put in, for we may need to dig out of the mud or grub up a stump on some trail that has never been traveled by a car. Yes, we shall need the axe, too, to cut firewood, or to use for any one of half a dozen purposes. The tool kit with a good assortment of tools is already in its proper place, and the axe and shovel have a special place behind the spare tire, for we shall need all the room inside the car.

Now, we shall load our supplies. First, we put in its regular place the bedroll; then the folding organ, for in so many places they do not have any musical instrument or hymnbooks; then the steel case well filled with Sunday School literature and tracts. We shall take the camera, for we may get some interesting pictures along the line. And we had better put in a first-aid kit; we may need it for ourselves or for someone else out there along the trail. We don't forget to put in that three-gallon canteen of water; we shall surely be needing it as we shall be making dry camp most of the time.

Now, we load the chuck box on the side of the car, to carry our provisions. First, we put in the cooking utensils including the dutch oven, for we shall have to bake our own bread. Then we want a steel grill for steaks, and stew pans and a wash basin. We need plenty of bacon, eggs, coffee, sugar, baking powder, flour, soda, salt, matches, both fresh and canned vegetables, a generous supply of fresh and dried fruits, some canned milk, and a pound of cheese.

That is all we need to take except a pile of good magazines we have gathered up to leave in the homes, and a supply of clothing the folks from back East sent, for we are going to see some mighty poor people on this trip. Many of them will suffer this winter unless someone helps them, and almost the only hope they have is in the Sunday School missionary.

Oh, yes, we want those teacher training books in order to get that class started over at Pine Ridge. Also, we had better take along some of those "Manuals" for weekday Bible instruction, for we want to enlist those schoolteachers in our district schools for weekday religious instruction. Those are the things with which we fill the car.

Here is a typical log of a Sunday School missionary:

104

Sixty miles along the highway, good roads; then took road out across the Black Mesa. Called all along the way. Arrived at Haynes Mines about 5:00 P.M. The folks had received my card and were delighted to see me. Made calls until the time for the service; stopped in at the shops, and it did my heart good to see how the men welcomed me. Said they would all be out for the service, and they were, too. Certainly had a fine service. They had a few new people in the camp who were so happy to be in a religious service. The little Sunday School is doing well, they told me, and they would like to start a teacher training class. Had a workers' conference with the teachers and officers after the service.

Drove back out in the canyon and am in camp here for the night. Have had a good supper for I was surely hungry. Now that the dishes are washed and a good fire going, I will write a letter or two and turn in for the night. It has been a good day. Called in ten homes, preached one sermon, held a workers' conference. Miles traveled — 190.

October 19

Was up early, had a good breakfast. Visited the school and made a talk to the kiddies. My, how my heart goes out for the little, lonely youngsters; they have so little. How they did listen as I told them the Bible story! I was there early and played some games with them before schooltime and they thought me a great fellow. I covet every one of them for the Kingdom! I must get in here next summer to conduct a vacation Bible School for them.

I stopped in to see Mr. James, who was hurt in an accident last week. Poor fellow, I am afraid there isn't much hope for him. His face beamed when I suggested we have a service. He said he guessed it would be the last one he would ever enjoy on this side of the River, as he felt sure he would be gone before I returned. He wanted me to know it would be all right. I hope I can get word in time, when he goes, to be here for the funeral. He has been a good man and should have a Christian burial.

I drove on through the mountains, visiting the homes along the way. Just after noon I saw a trail leading off to the left and I felt I just had to follow it to see where it led. After about two miles, it turned off up a canyon, and three miles farther I saw a little log house over at the foot of a big cliff. I went up, knocked at the door, and from the back of the house came a very elderly woman. When I told her who I was and why I stopped, she looked out over my shoulder to the high, snow-covered, mountain peak and repeated a part of the Eighty-Fourth Psalm: "How amiable are thy Tabernacles, O Lord of Hosts! My soul longeth, yea, even fainteth for the courts of the Lord! My heart and my flesh crieth out for the Living God."

Then she said, "I have lived here for more than twenty-seven years, and every day I have come here to the door and repeated those words. I guess I've said them ten thousand times. And now you come! The Lord bless you, my man, won't you come in?"

And what a wonderful visit we had. By and by her daughter, son-in-law, and granddaughter came in. And when along toward evening I would go, they said, "No, you can't go. You must spend the night with us; we have never had a minister in our home."

After the evening meal, we sat together before the open fire. It was not long until the conversation turned to religion and God. The son-in-law said, "It must be a wonderful thing to be a Christian." I said, "Yes, it is the most wonderful thing I know anything about."

He said he did not know much about it as he was born near there and had heard only a few sermons in his life. He said he had never prayed a prayer in his life and would not know how. I suggested that we have prayer before we said good night, so a message was read from the Book, and then we knelt there at midnight and I led in prayer. As I

106

prayed, I heard him sob as only a big, whole-hearted, honest soul can sob. When I was through with my prayer, I said to him, "Don't you feel like you would like to pray right now?" He prayed a most wonderful prayer. When we arose from our prayers together, the husband put his arm around his wife and said to her, "Let us accept Christ, as Mr. Hall suggested, and be Christian people and have a Christian home." Their daughter rushed up and said, "Me, too, Daddy," and so the three of them made their confession of faith to me in the presence of the elderly lady. Once more I led in a prayer of thanksgiving to God and asked Him to be with them, blessing and helping them all the days of their lives.

It has been a good day. Miles — 43. Eight families visited, three conversions, one school talk.

October 20

I drove ten miles, and came across the Bar-Y cowboys rounding up their beef steers. They gave me a horse and I spent the day with them riding like a trooper. They were mighty glad to see me; like so many ranch crews, they were shorthanded and needed help badly.

They thought they would have some fun in the afternoon when they gave me that "Dynamite" horse to ride. I guess the Lord must have been with me, for I was able to stay on top. Anyway, it gave me an opportunity to win their admiration. Then when we gathered about the fire after supper for the service, they listened to me as I preached. It was great to preach to them out there by the glow of the campfire. When I left them they begged me to come back soon. It is late — I drove on forty miles to camp. Sixty miles today, five visits, one sermon.

Sunday, October 21

Well, this has been a very blessed day. I was up early and drove fifty miles to Lone Pine Springs to our little new

107

chapel. When I arrived about nine o'clock, I found some of the folks already there. They had driven in yesterday and camped in order to be on time, for they had a long way to come.

I had organized the Sunday School at Lone Pine Springs a year ago when they had no place to meet except in homes or out under trees. They said to me on my last visit that they would have a big surprise for me when I came back next time.

I had wondered what the surprise might be, and this was it. They had decided they would make an old abandoned mud house into a church. They had moved a window from another abandoned house, picked up scraps here and there, and built their little place of worship, and they wanted me to dedicate it.

I was astonished at what a good job they had done, with so little. It was neat and attractive as well.

I asked them whether it was free of debt and ready to dedicate. They said "Yes, it is all paid for."

"How much did it cost?"

"A dime."

I looked about to see where they had spent the dime, but couldn't find it. They said they had bought a dime's worth of nails to put the door jambs in place.

We had Sunday School, and a fine school it was. Then I preached for them. After a big fire was built and coffee made, all spread their lunch together, and I never saw so much to eat nor such a long table.

Before all were finished with their lunch I heard someone playing the organ and singing. How these folks do love to sing! I won't ever forget Mrs. Evans coming to me and, with tears in her eyes, telling me that I would never know how much she had enjoyed the little organ; it had been twelve years since she had heard the tones of a musical instrument. Then I preached again, and thought that would be all for the day, but they begged me to preach the third sermon, which I did.

108

After that I called together the Sunday School teachers and officers for a workers' conference. When we were through with that the folks said they had plenty of food left for supper and that we would all eat, and then I could preach again. I preached the strongest evangelistic sermon I knew how. There were fourteen who made a public profession of their faith in Christ.

I thought I would never get away. Some said if they lived to be a thousand years old they would never forget the day. Finally, the last good-bye was said, and I drove out here in the canyon, tired but happy. Thank God for a church that sends out missionaries to these people in our own land!

I am camped tonight in a beautiful forest. There isn't a human being within ten miles of me, so far as I know. It is so still and quiet you can almost feel it, and yet I hear many strange voices of the forest and the night. Over the hill comes the lonely call of the coyote, and up in the trees I hear the hoot of an old owl that seems to be watching over me. The fire burns low, and there is a chill in the air — I will have frost on my tarpaulin in the morning. As I have a long drive tomorrow, I am going to turn my face to the stars for a good sleep. There is a great peace in my heart and I thank God for the joy of being a missionary in this great mission field. Sixty miles, four sermons, fourteen conversions.

October 22

I didn't get as far today as I had expected. I found a new schoolhouse, stopped to visit, and they persuaded me to stay over and preach for them tonight. I called on all the folks and everyone was at the service.

The folks wanted a Sunday School, and we organized one with twenty-four enrolled. The teacher also agreed to use our manual of weekday Bible instruction.

I had to drive about sixty miles after the service in order to get to La Mesa tomorrow night to begin the meetings

109

there. I wish I had another day to spend along through this country. I didn't know so many people lived here.

I traveled 120 miles, made thirteen calls, spoke to the school children, preached one sermon, and organized a Sunday School.

Sunday, November 4

Have been here since Tuesday and the folks were certainly glad to see me. They had not heard a sermon in twenty-three months. It is hard to get into this country because it is so isolated and the roads are terrible. To reach here I had to climb up over three mountain passes of more than a thousand feet altitude, and drive over very muddy roads. Had to dig out several times, build two temporary bridges, and do a lot of road work. Gasoline is high, too; it costs thirty-five cents a gallon.

We have had a fine time this week. I was sorry to have to close the services tonight. They begged so hard for me to stay on but I must keep my schedule. Have two more weeks on this trip before I reach home. Have slept in my bedroll every night except one. And, my, how it has rained the last two nights!

I don't know what to do about the church organization. We have had twenty-eight conversions this week and these new Christians are so anxious to join the church. They begged me to organize a church, and handed me a petition with about thirty names on it. They will all come in, forgetting about their particular denominational affiliations; but if we organize, how can we care for them? There isn't another church within fifty miles that they could join.

If only we had more money to provide additional missionaries! It seems that our work will never be done. We must appeal to our churches — on behalf of the board, on behalf of our Lord, on behalf of these people — for more money to carry on our Lord's work.

110

Then, too, I hope more of our fine young people will dedicate their lives definitely to the cause of national missions. One's life counts for so much out in these great mission fields.

Report to Supporting Churches

1941

Dear Friends:

ALONE IN CAMP for a day and night, I have been looking back through the old year and facing the new. In retrospect I travel back along memory's road through 1940, and experience a mingled feeling of rejoicing and regret: Rejoicing in many glorious experiences, and regret that we have failed to reach many goals we had set for the year. For all the failures and mistakes we can only ask God's forgiveness through his great mercy, and turn our faces to the days ahead.

As I think of the old year, many happy experiences come before me — painting pictures of groups, large and small, gathered in small schoolhouses, and chapels, in out-of-the-way homes and out under the trees, all asking the way of life. These pictures I can never erase from my mind. It has been a blessed year in the work of our Lord.

The summer's work was perhaps the most outstanding. On May 27 we left home with a two-ton Dodge truck pulling a four-wheel chuckwagon trailer made for this purpose. It was loaded with large cooking vessels — five, ten, and twenty gallon pots and kettles, extra large dutch ovens for cooking roasts and baking bread; enough tin plates, cups, knives, forks and spoons to serve up to a thousand people at one time; plus groceries and all necessary things for setting up a complete camp in the forest for about a hundred young people.

After traveling 457 miles we came to our first campsite for one of our conferences, a beautiful place in the Graham Mountains of southern Arizona, way down on the Mexican border. There a fine group of young people met us, and for six days we lived, studied and worshipped in a blessed fellowship. The days were very full and happy with Bible study, learning how to live and walk in Christ's way, learning somethng about the great work of missions in the wide world, and worship periods out under the trees — and, of course, there was time for play and fellowship.

We hated to leave, but we had to move on. So like a circus crew we broke camp and headed with the truck back across the hills and mountains some 200 miles to the Black Range Mountains of New Mexico. Nearly a hundred young people greeted us, and after six days with them, we were once more on the move over high and treacherous mountain roads, 185 miles to a beautiful spot in the Mogollon Mountains where we met another fine group for six more happy and blessed days.

Reluctantly we again said good-bye and headed over the the mountains for Albuquerque. It was now time to be off on the traveling seminar arranged by our Board of National Missions.

A couple of days we spent in making up fifty-six bedrolls, and loading three trucks with all the camping equipment and provisions we would need to take care of fifty new campers, people who had never spent a night in the open in their lives.

Our guests were folks from our larger churches in the distant parts of the nation. They had traveled far and

113

were willing to undergo the hardships of pioneer camp life, sleep on the ground in bedrolls, eat all meals prepared and cooked by the missionaries over the open campfire, and bump along dim and rough trails, in order to see something of our national mission fields.

We made up quite a caravan: the three trucks, ten cars, and fifty-six people in all. It was a big job to get everything together, make it portable, pack it away, set up and tear down the camp, cook and serve three meals a day, and still travel some two hundred miles in between. All such things as water, food and often wood had to be hauled right along with us.

What an excellent group they were and how quickly they adjusted themselves to pioneer camping, with never a complaint. They were a great inspiration to those of us who had the privilege of traveling with them, and to the missionaries we visited in the various mission stations. Our trip took us over some two thousand miles of New Mexico and Arizona, and we were out eleven days. It was a happy and inspiring trip.

We found ourselves back in Albuquerque by July 8. After reloading the truck we headed north and west over desert and plain for some 260 miles to reach the beautiful Spruce Haven Canyon in the high mountains of southwestern Colorado. There we found nearly a hundred young people to spend six days with us. Such eagerness to learn about the things of the Kingdom was manifested by the youth of that section, so many of them making a profession of their faith in the Lord Jesus. But once more it was time to move on, so back across the mesas, and up on the side of beautiful Storm Mountain. A hundred and sixty miles away we set up our camp once more with the same happy results. A night's trip back into Albuquerque followed, to see loved ones at home and prepare to leave again.

Now it was time to try out a new experiment, a Ranchmen's Camp Meeting. With the truck and car loaded to fullest capacity, we headed south and east for 180 miles to beautiful Nogal Mesa. Not much advertising had been done. Word has been passed along from cowboy to cowboy and from ranch to ranch that some of us were going up to Nogal Mesa for a few days of fellowship and prayer — and of course there would be some preaching, too.

There is a sparsely settled country, where the ranches are far apart. We had hoped and prayed that we might have as many as a hundred people. We were very happy to find that many were there for their very first service and the closing day we fed more than seven hundred. It was one of life's happiest experiences.

The cowboys came with their families from far and near, some traveling more than 250 miles to be present. They put up their tents, and with our camp conference equipment we set up an open-air kitchen and all ate at the central camp. Two cooks were employed, and with volunteer help from the cowboys, the crowd was fed three times a day. About seven hundred were fed in a little over an hour the last day. Five whole beeves were consumed in five days, all cooked over the open fire.

A large tent was stretched up in a beautiful spot for a place of worship. The cowboys pretty largely set up the program. Five services were arranged for each day — preaching service at 9:00 A.M. and 2:30 P.M., two prayer meetings at 4:30 P.M., and a preaching service in the evening.

The men's prayer meeting was especially fine. This was a laymen's meeting, no preachers allowed, and the cowboys led the meetings themselves. Every man and boy on the grounds attended and with the exception of two boys all took some part. The meeting was held under a beautiful juniper tree that is very sacred to the cowboys who attended these meetings.

It would have thrilled the heart of any Christian to have been with us in those closing services when whole families came forward to make public profession of their faith in our Lord. Dr. King of our Board of National Missions did most of the preaching, and how the people did learn to love him and the messages he brought.

Wherever I go even now I hear echoes of those days spent together on Nogal Mesa. I have just heard of one family living way back on a lonely ranch, who, as a result of the camp meeting, are going into Roswell, seventy-five miles from their ranch, to join the church. People are constantly saying to me that it is the greatest thing that ever happened in New Mexico.

A hardheaded businessmen's club, in a town some distance away, wrote a letter saying that it meant more than anything that had ever happened in that part of the country and urging us to carry it on through the years.

After the glorious experience on Nogal Mesa, we once more started out on a thousand mile trip into southeastern Wyoming where we set up and enjoyed another fine young people's conference. From there we traveled on into the Black Hills of South Dakota for our last camp conference of the summer, and were just able to get home by the first of September.

Yes, we were tired and worn after being out from May 27, sleeping on the ground all summer with the exception of three or four nights, working with the various camps, cooking, preaching and teaching. But there was a great feeling of peace and satisfaction as we unloaded the truck and stored away the equipment, to wait until the last of May when we will start on another tour for the sake of the neglected youth out here in this great Southwest country and for the glory of our Lord's name.

Although the forests are still covered with snow and winter winds sweep across the mountains, I feel the urge to get out the truck and camp equipment, and head out across to the places of quiet retreat, in the temples of God's own making — there to meet our many young friends, and once more lead them in the worship of Christ, the King.

The youth we reached last summer through our camp conferences were not the young people from our organized churches for the most part, but from isolated ranches, homesteads, mining and lumber camps, who do not enjoy the fellowship of other young people often, and who have the privileges of Christian services, only when one of the Sunday School missionaries can get around to their homes or communities for a service.

More than five hundred different young people spent a week in camp with us, besides the seminar and camp meeting. What this week meant to these fine young people cannot be measured. A great many of them made a profession of their faith in our Lord, accepting Him as their Savior and going back to their homes to live for Him. Thank God for the opportunity of working with them.

This is only a glimpse of the work through the summer. A great deal could be said for the work through the fall, winter and spring months, but space does not permit me to mention all of it. There are wonderful experiences of dedicating chapels, organizing churches and Sunday Schools, special evangelistic services and many other worthwhile activities.

In humility I bow before my gracious Lord, and say to Him, "Take my life, and let it consecrated be." To Him be all the honor and glory.

Looking forward to another year of happy service in His name,

Sincerely,
Ralph J. Hall

It has been wonderful to have the support and interest of several churches in my ministry. The month I entered the field of Sunday School missions in 1923, the Sunday School of the First Presbyterian Church in Haddonfield, New Jersey, adopted me as their missionary. How much it has meant through the years to have their prayers, interest and support. I have been back to visit them at least thirty different times. I have spoken from the pulpit there several times, and have spoken to the Sunday School and to every other organization in the church. Always I will be grateful for their love and support.

Several churches have had a special interest in us as a family and in supporting our mission: East Liberty Presbyterian Church in Pittsburg, Pennsylvania; old First Presbyterian Church in downtown Pittsburgh; Collingwood Avenue Sunday School, Toledo, Ohio; Westmont Presbyterian Church, Johnstown, Pennsylvania; Central-Brick Presbyterian Church in East Orange, New Jersey; and many others with which we have had very close relationships. To all I say a hearty thank you for your interest, help and support.

The Lady from Philadelphia

OFTEN I WOULD GET WORD from the board
that someone from the East or West wanted to see
something of our work and would like to travel with
me for a few days, living as I lived, to see me on the job.
On one occasion I learned that a Mrs. Jones from Philadelphia would arrive in a couple of days and wanted to
spend the weekend; I was told not to change any plans, just
let her ride along and observe.

She was a wealthy and wonderful woman, and a good
sport as well.

I had a trip planned to the southwestern part of the
state. When she arrived I had the car all loaded — chuck
box, Billhorn folding organ, bedrolls. I took along a cot
for her, too, for I knew the homes in which we would be
staying had no spare beds and rooms.

We drove on along our way having a good time visiting.
She was a small, dainty woman, perhaps seventy years of
age, but much interested in how I lived in camp. She kept
saying, "I wish something would happen so we'd have to
camp. I sure would like to sleep right out in the wilds under
the open sky." Just before sunset I pulled off the road, built
a fire, broiled steaks, and made dutch oven biscuits, and a

119

pot of coffee. She ate as though that plain food was from the finest restaurant. As soon as I could, we got started again; we had some sixty-five miles to travel before reaching Reserve where she was to sleep in the manse with the young couple who had just arrived to take over the work there.

Over in the west above the mountains dark and angry storm clouds were gathering; soon great flashes of lightning and loud thunder claps issued their warnings. Shortly it was pouring rain. We were traveling a dirt road and began slipping and sliding every which way. Some sharp mountain curves kept her clinging to the car door and sometimes smothering a scream. But she said, "Don't worry about me. I can take anything."

Soon the brunt of the storm was over and as we drove on she kept saying, "What a thrilling experience."

After several miles of sloshing through the mud we topped a hill and in the distance we could see the lights of Reserve. Instead of being glad that the ride was over, she said, "Aw shucks. Now I'll have to go in a house and sleep just like always."

I said, "Don't be too sure, Mrs. Jones, we aren't there yet." I knew we had to cross the Frisco River and I knew that rain had fallen up at the headwaters a few miles on and that most likely the river would be on a wild rampage.

Sure enough, as we approached it I saw that it was indeed wild. I drove up to the edge and stopped to look the situation over. It would have taken a good boat to cross it.

Mrs. Jones said, "Now what will we do?"

"We will do what you have been wishing for all afternoon," I said. "We'll sleep under the open sky."

I turned out the car lights for a minute to get a better look at the clouds building once more above us. It was pitch dark and she became very frightened: "Oh, it's so dark. I don't think I ever saw it so black. Always there have been streetlights or something."

I put on the lights and backed away, then pulled off to

the side of the road and stopped. She asked, "What are we going to do?"

I said, "We're going to bed for a wonderful night's sleep out here in the open."

She said, "Oh no, I can't do that." Then in a stern voice: "Now, Hall, I demand that you get me to a hotel or someplace out of this dreadful storm and darkness."

I told her I could by driving back along that crooked muddy road we had just traveled.

"You didn't like the road then and it is worse by now. Do you want to do that?"

She said no.

I reminded her that she was in New Mexico range country and not Pennsylvania.

"Well," she said, "I will just sit in the car and you can lock it so nothing can get to me, and I'll make the best of it."

I didn't argue with her then, but got out and fixed her cot and bedroll right along beside the car. Then by much pleading and reasoning I got her to agree to try it. I got her bag for her and told her to undress and slip into the bedroll, after which I would come and fix her waterproof tarp so she wouldn't get wet, since I was sure the rain was not over.

She asked, "I shouldn't undress, should I?"

I said, "Sure, get ready for bed as always."

"Well, how much should I-er-er undress?"

I said, "All the way down. Get comfortable and you'll have a wonderful sleep."

Pretty soon she was in bed and I began telling her about the country and the people. Presently there was no answer from her. In a few minutes you never heard such snores coming from a little woman.

It rained hard in the night, but I heard not a thing from her. As day began to break I got up, built a fire, and put on the coffee pot. Still no sound from Mrs. Jones.

121

I began to get uneasy about her, so I walked over to the car and opened and slammed the door.

A scream: "Mr. Hall! Mr. Hall!"

"Good morning, Mrs. Jones," I said. "Breakfast is about ready. Come and get it."

In a little while she joined me for coffee, bacon and eggs, and hot dutch oven biscuits, the most charming and happy little old lady you ever saw.

How thrilled she was over living through that experience! She insisted on sleeping in the bedroll every night. She did a lot of speaking for the Board. I met her several times after that in the East, and she never tired of talking about her wild, western trip and the thrilling experience of living among national missionaries.

Embarrassing Moments

LIFE HAS ITS EMBARRASSING MOMENTS, and I have had more than my share, I think. In 1934 I was asked to speak at the Florida Chain of Missionary Assemblies, sponsored by the Women's Council of Missions (Interdenominational). We had a team of twelve people from the mission fields around the world — such outstanding people as E. Stanley Jones, John R. Mott, and Dr. Harold Storm of Arabia. For a month we toured all of Florida, speaking on the radio, in big mass meetings, at colleges and universities, and service clubs.

Each of us was asked to submit five main addresses for special groups, and we were urged to make the addresses as submitted. If we were to speak before service clubs, we were to make the same address to each one. I averaged five addresses a day for thirty days and I seemed to always feel good and to be able to pinch hit for anyone who could not make his or her appointment.

On one occasion I came back to our hotel, after speaking to a college group, at about 11:00 A.M. Miss Woodford, our manager, was waiting for me at the door. She told me they were having a big district meeting of the Kiwanis Club at Frost Bite, some sixty miles away. The national president

123

had been due to speak but was in an auto accident and she had told them she would send a speaker to substitute for him. They were meeting at twelve o'clock.

She said, "You'll have to hurry. We have a chauffeur and Cadillac car waiting for you at the door. Go now."

We made that sixty miles mighty fast. But when I got there the presiding officer said, "We're through eating. Will you speak now and eat later?"

I was about to cave in, but said, "O.K."

I had planned to use the same address I used at all the service clubs, as requested, so I wasn't worried about what I would say. He gave me a very elaborate introduction, saying he had heard me several times and I never repeated myself. (He had heard me speaking to different groups.) Then he added, "I greatly enjoyed hearing Mr. Hall yesterday on the radio as I'm sure most of you did when he spoke to the club in Winter Haven. I know you will enjoy him today. I give you Mr. Hall."

I had not known the address the day before had been broadcast; there had been a big bouquet of flowers in front of me, and the microphone must have been in those flowers.

I sure did have to take off in a different direction from what I had planned. I guess I got away with it, but for the moment I was flabbergasted.

On another occasion I was called from New York by the Promotion Department of National Missions and told to stop on my way East where I was going to do some promotion work for a month. I was a little excited over being called long distance from New York. I always said "Yes" to anything the Board asked me to do, so I said, "All right, I'll be there."

Then I began to think of all the caller had said. The stopover was a big church in Buffalo for a great city-wide rally of more than four hundred men. I was to substitute for no less a person than Dr. Robert E. Speer. Then I got scared.

124

I barely had time to make my train, got into Chicago on a late train, almost missed my connection, and got on the wrong train headed for Detroit instead of Buffalo. By running I caught the train for Buffalo and arrived there late, barely in time for the supper meeting, and in a bad blizzard. I did manage to get a taxi and told the driver to rush me to the church.

As I went into the great Fellowship Hall where the meeting was to be, and saw that crowd of men, I thought how disappointed they were going to be when they would not hear Dr. Speer and how poor a substitute I would be for him.

The men were all greeting each other, but nobody said, "Hello, Preacher" as the people called me on the range. I knew not one man in Buffalo. All at once I became very lonesome, and I never wanted to be home so bad in my life.

While I was pulling off my overcoat I overheard two men talking. One of them said to the other, "Has your speaker shown up yet?" The other replied, "No, he hasn't and I am getting a little worried." The first fellow said, "I hope we don't have to have another bad one. We've had some awful flat tires in these outside speakers lately. I'm fed up with them."

The other man agreed that they had been saddled with some flops and said "Well, we have a good quartet and I have put a little stuff together, so I guess we can get by okay." However, as he turned away he said over his shoulder, "They say though that this young fellow from New Mexico is very good." To which his friend replied, "I saw his picture and he sure doesn't look like much to me." This did not help my feelings very much.

Just then they called us all into the dining room, a beautiful room with gorgeous tables. I just pushed along with the crowd and found myself a seat at a table way in the back of the room. I looked up front and there was a high platform with the speakers' table. I noticed one chair turned against the table and knew they were saving it for me. I didn't feel I had the courage to go up there and take it.

I thought I would make myself known to the man I was sitting by, so I asked if he lived in Buffalo. He said his home was only a few blocks from the church. I told him my name was Ralph Hall and I lived in New Mexico, thinking sure he would say, "Oh yes, you are our speaker." He merely said, "Glad to have you with us," and turned to visit with his neighbor on the other side of him; that was the last I heard from him.

I was at the end of the table so had no one to talk with down that way. The table was a wide one and the fellow across from me was busily talking with his neighbor. I tried to butt in by remarking that it was a very cold and stormy night, and we did not have storms like that down in NEW MEXICO. He was not interested in the kind of weather we had in New Mexico.

I noticed the chair was still vacant up there at the head table. The main course was served and the quartet sang a number. I knew I had to make myself known; the Board had sent me there to speak. I was sure homesick.

The young women of the church were serving the tables. When one came to take my plate away, I told her who I was and that I was supposed to speak, and asked her if she would tell them at the head table that I was there when they got ready for me. She was most gracious and said she would go at once. I saw her make for the table up on that high platform and talk to the man I had overheard talking when I came in. She pointed back my way and he came rushing down. He greeted me cordially but bawled me out for not looking him up. I took that vacant chair.

When it was time for him to introduce me, what a whale of a job he did. You would think the angel Gabriel had arrived.

I was scared and felt out of place. Before I realized what I was doing I was telling them of the very interesting conversation I had overheard and how sorry I felt for them.

126

The whole group stood up and gave me a rousing ovation.
What a wonderful group they were. I had a delightful
time and often was asked to speak to them in later years.

Black Mesa

1929

I NEVER HAVE BEEN ABLE to travel over the western range country, whether by car or horseback, and see a dim road or trail turning off without feeling a longing in my heart to follow that trail and see where it will lead me. I have followed a great many of them. Almost every time it has led me to some isolated family, mining camp, timber camp, or cow camp, but always to people. At the end of many of the trails I have been led into unexpected and rich experiences where I could be of service.

Following one trail on one occasion I saw at the end of it a little shack, typical of the homestead country. When I knocked at the door of that little home I was met at the door by a rather young woman. I didn't have to ask if all was well; I knew it was not. I don't think I have ever seen sorrow and suffering so deeply written on a face.

When I told her who I was and why I had stopped, she turned a little and just stood there with a faraway look in her eyes, gazing out across the prairie, seemingly forgetting all about me. The she said, "I beg your pardon. Won't you come in?" I sat down and she walked over to the one

128

little window in the room; she stood there with her body rigid and taut, almost a statue, gazing out across the Black Mesa. Presently I saw her body relax, and dropping her head down on her folded arms on the windowsill, she wept as I have heard few people weep.

When she was exhausted, I asked, "What is wrong? What has happened? Can you tell me about it."

She said, "Look out the window." I walked over and looked out. There was nothing to see stretching to the horizon in the distance, except out there about a mile from the home stood a little stunted tree. "It's out there," she said, "the little grave."

Then came tumbling from her lips the sad story of their little daughter, three years of age, how she had been bitten by a large rattlesnake and had died almost immediately. She looked at me and asked, "Oh, why didn't you come sooner, a week sooner? Why did you wait so long?"

It was just a week ago that day that they had buried their little darling. She told how gracious and kind the neighbors had been as they made the little box, and how the women had padded it and lined it with beautiful cloth.

"I think I could stand it," she said, "if only we could have had a minister and we could have given her a Christian burial."

Then she thought of something I had not as she asked, "Won't you go up there with us and say a few words and say a prayer?" Of course I said I would.

Presently the husband came and she told him what she had asked me to do. He said, "Wonderful. Can we ask some of the neighbors to come in and go with us?" I said, "Sure."

Two of the neighbor girls, about fifteen years of age, saddled their horses and rode miles over the mesa to a little spring where they found some evergreens and wild flowers. Just at evening time a small group of us went up to the little grave.

It was one of the loneliest moments I have experienced as we stood there in the lengthening shadows of the evening

129

time, beside this little lonely grave covered with evergreens and tiny wild flowers. I counted it a great privilege to say a few words of comfort and to offer a prayer for the bereaved family. How very much it meant to that lonely mother.

Moving Pictures

IN 1929 I WAS TOLD by the Board that they were sending the Reverend Fred Thorne down for five days to
make a moving picture of the work of Sunday School
missions in New Mexico. Fred came in August, at the height
of the rainy season. After he told me something of what he
wanted to get, I called Roger Sherman and we packed the
old Ford with bedrolls, chuck box, camera equipment, and
umbrellas to hold over the camera. For the next five days
we put in sixteen hours a day, traveling many hundreds of
miles. It rained on us day and night. We were bogged down
in mud and plagued by flooded arroyos. In spite of it all,
by the end of the five days we had about a thousand feet of
usable film made.

The result was called "The Vanishing Frontier." The
picture was widely used throughout the whole church. Copies
are still available. I was in the Union Station (railroad) in
1931 when a young fellow who had been watching me and
following me about, finally came up to me and said, "Aren't
you a moving picture star?"

I thanked him and said, "No."

"Well," he said, "you are, too. I saw you in a picture
last Sunday evening in our church."

In the late forties Fred Thorne came back and traveled with us for six weeks, making another picture of the camp meetings and youth camps. This was far different from the making of the first film, when we just had the camera and umbrellas. Fred had about a thousand pounds of equipment, and made the picture in color. It is called the "Cowboys Hitching Post" and is still being used in the churches. We did not have sound equipment with us, but the film was narrated by a professional voice.

About 1955, Fred Thorne came back to make another short film called "Altars of God." Dr. Louis Evans was with us for this one; Fred had the sound equipment along on this trip and it was used on the spot.

I'm afraid most of the "actors" were not too good at the job, but we were all glad for others to see something of the work to be done out here in the West.

Valley View

1928

ONE OF THE MOST DIFFICULT THINGS for me in those early days was to have to say to people, "I'm sorry, but I can't come."

Always there was that urgent plea, "When will you come back? When can we look for you again?"

I would take out that little notebook and look over the schedule for the months ahead. Oftentimes I would have to say to them, "I'll be back within six months," or "I'll be back next year." It was painful to see the disappointed look on their faces, but always there was the assurance that all of us in the mission work gave, that we would come back as soon as we could.

I remember on one occasion down at Valley View when the folks gathered around and said, "Will you come back next month?"

I had to say to them "I'll be back in about six months."

They said, "Oh, will we have to wait that long?"

"I'll come as soon as I can," I said.

And so at the end of about six months I had written giving them the day when I would be there. As I drove down that way, on the day before I had promised to be there, I thought I would camp near the schoolhouse on the flats. When I drove just at dark up to the schoolhouse I saw the light of a campfire. I drew nearer and saw crowds of people gathered around. As I drove up they came rushing up and pulled the car door open. I don't know whether a king ever received a more cordial welcome.

I said to them, "What are you doing here tonight? The services, you know, are not until tomorrow."

"Well," they said, "we had an idea that you would come here to the schoolhouse to camp and we just wanted to be here to say welcome. Come on over, supper's ready."

Everything that loving hands and loving hearts could do had been done to make this table attractive and food tasty. And so in good fellowship we shared our evening meal together.

I remember walking over to the campfire and picking up the old, black, hot coffee pot to get that extra cup of coffee; just as I did, some fellow came up and gave me a slap on the back that almost knocked me in the fire and spilled hot coffee on my hands. I looked around and he said, "You don't know me, do you?"

I looked into his face, and said "No, but I've seen you. Where is your range?"

"Why, Preach," he said, "don't you remember that night down on the Alaweco?"

"Why, yes. Sure, Bill, I remember." And I asked, "How is everything?"

And old Bill said, "Everything is all right."

I remember that night when, at their earnest request, I had gone up to the chuck wagon to take a tin cup from the chuck box and draw a cup of water out of that old water keg on the side of the chuck wagon. There I had baptized this man and two others who stood there with bowed heads. It had been one of those beautiful nights when the moon shone in all its splendor and seemed to fill the earth with the glory of God.

Bill interrupted my thoughts. "Come on over and meet the family," he said. "I have always said to them if that fellow ever comes near the ranch I want you to meet him and I want you to hear him."

I asked, "Where do you live, Bill?"

"Oh," he said, "over there in the Graham Mountains."

I looked yonder at the mountains across in Arizona and said, "How far?"

"Well," he replied, "I guess an old crow would make it in about 100 miles. We made it in 150."

And then the folks said, "Preach, we're here and we don't have to hurry home. Couldn't we just have a service before we go?" So we all gathered there around the smoldering fire that had cooked the evening meal, and I preached for them.

That place, and those people, were to me a stronger inspiration to preach than the finest pulpit or the grandest sanctuary.

Soon after the organizing of the Sunday School at Valley View, the people there sent a petition to the Rio Grande Presbytery asking to be organized into a church. The presbytery acted favorably and appointed an organizing commission.

All preparations were made and the day came for which they had so eagerly waited. We were to have Sunday School, followed by the worship service and the organization of the church. There was not even standing room in the little schoolhouse. It was my true pleasure to preach the sermon.

For me, and I am sure for all the people, it was a rare and impressive service. The members were all enrolled, many coming in by profession of their faith in the Lord Jesus Christ as their Savior. I think it was seventeen that I baptized. Some came by reaffirmation of their faith, having been so long away from the church where they had been members that they could not obtain letters of tranfer. Others came with letters of transfer. We proceeded to elect the officers of the church and to ordain and install them, closing with a prayer of dedication and thanksgiving.

They had planned to have dinner on the grounds and an afternoon service, so everyone had brought baskets of food. The tables were spread and we had a sumptuous dinner with wonderful fellowship around the tables.

While we were eating, one of the ladies asked if she could speak to me alone. We walked out to her family's wagon and she said, "Mr. Hall, you have said nothing about a communion service. I thought sure we would have a communion service on this first day of our new church. It's been so long since we've had the privilege of sitting down for a communion service. We were talking this morning and remembered it had been nearly twenty years."

I told her how sorry I was that we had not planned such a service, and that we didn't have the elements.

"There must be someway we can arrange it," she said. After a few moments of thought she said, "Oh, I know what we can do. I have a large jar of canned raspberries that has not been opened. Can't we strain them and use the juice for wine? And we can use bread from the table, can't we?"

I replied, "Yes, we can."

I will never forget taking that jar of berries to my car and straining them through the corner of a clean tea towel.

Not thinking of the communion service, no one had brought linen for the table, which was the teacher's desk. I had in my chuck box a roll of homemade tea towels that a group of women from one of the eastern churches had sent me. They were new and freshly pressed and large, made for use when serving at big camp dinners.

The table was prepared by loving hands, using plates and cups from my chuck box. I had a short conference with the two elders newly ordained and installed; they had never before served communion.

When the time came we all gathered once more in the

136

crowded schoolroom. After the sermon we had the most memorable communion service I have ever attended. The new elders came forward and I don't think I ever saw elders serve with more dignity and reverence. After the last person had been served, I covered the table once more with the tea towels. The last rays of the Sabbath sun were falling through the windows and across the communion table. We sang a hymn and went out. It was one of those holy and sacred hours never to be forgotten. There was hardly a dry eye in the room.

After they had said affectionate good-byes, and had urged me to come back soon, I got in my car and drove out of the valley. I stopped at the top of the ridge, and looked at the wagons, buggies and cars of people traveling toward their homes. Many had said, as they tried to thank me, "We'll never forget this day." I knew they were traveling home with a new joy and gladness in their hearts. In the heart of this Sunday School missionary there was a great joy and gratitude to my God for another blessed day spent in such work and with such people.

Report to New Mexico Synod

1937

IT WAS ALWAYS A SPECIAL PLEASURE to speak to the Synod of New Mexico, where there were so many close friends and co-workers. This is part of such a speech, in 1937:

The year 1937 marks the fiftieth anniversary of the inauguration of the Sunday School extension work of the Presbyterian church. Through these fifty years more than three million children have received Christian training in these mission Sunday Schools. In upwards of 2,300 communities, Presbyterian churches have grown out of these Bible Schools established by Sunday School missionaries. It is fitting that we pause for a moment to pay homage to the great missionaries of our church, who blazed the trail. I am sure I speak the deep sentiment of all of my fellow workers today when I say we feel very humble as the mantle of the heroes falls upon our shoulders. . . .

We are 110 in number today, and we are out under the same charter and with the same great commission. Through the years we have lost no part of that program, but rather it has been enlarged to keep pace with and to embrace modern methods of Christian training and education. There

138

are still vast unchurched areas that must be reached, and thousands and millions of young lives to be trained for His service. We are maintaining some 3,000 mission Sunday Schools as permanent institutions. In each of these more must be done than the conducting of a brief session of Sunday School on the Sabbath day. Leaders must be trained, classes in Bible study planned and carried through. Weekday activities must be carried on for the training of these young lives for Christian service.

Last summer about 2,000 vacation Bible Schools were conducted, reaching some 100,000 lives. Who can estimate the value of these hours and days of Bible study by these 100,000 young people?

The program of weekday Bible instruction is carried on chiefly by the rural schoolteachers with the help of the Sunday School missionaries. Last summer 8,000 schoolteachers caught the vision and touched some 200,000 young lives through the weekday Bible classes.

There is also the work through the young people's societies organized and maintained by the Sunday School missionaries. And there are the community Bible classes conducted through the week, as well as a course in teacher training in almost every mission Sunday School. . . .

In the closing moments, let us look at our own field here in New Mexico. One day about twelve years ago two Sunday School missionaries met by appointment in a lovely mountain valley in southwestern New Mexico. They were the Reverend J. D. Henry (the honored and loved missionary who spent so many years in the service of our Lord) and myself. We had just completed a partial survey of the mission fields of the state. We drew a map of the state and located the fields we were serving and then the possible fields. We were appalled by the needs.

After two days of earnest study and planning, we knelt down out there under the stars at an early morning hour and dedicated our lives anew to the great task of taking the Gospel through the Sunday Schools to New Mexico. Soon we parted, with a great faith to undertake this gigantic task. Many have been the meetings since then to plan, to study, to give thanks to Almighty God and to rededicate our lives to this great cause.

We have cause for great rejoicing, for God and our Board of National Missions have been very kind to us. Today, sixteen of these Bible schools have grown into church organizations. Twelve of them have church buildings. Instead of the two of us covering the whole field, we now have eleven men. Eight of them are commissioned as Sunday School missionaries. Two of them receive a part of their support through the synod's budget of National Missions. Three of the eleven receive their support through the local churches' and synod budgets.

Time forbids me going into detail regarding the progress of the work and the coming of the various men, but perhaps you will be interested in knowing who these men are and where they are serving:

Mr. Kuykendall was the first to come, and after serving a large field from Silver City to Magdalena for some time, he is now living in Silver City and serving a field reaching from the Mexican border to Mogollon in the Mogollon Mountains. It is a large field with a number of new Sunday Schools.

Mr. Marquis is serving points in southwestern New Mexico and southern Arizona, a large and difficult field. Mr. Champlin is living in Reserve and serving the western part of the state, reaching as far east as Magdalena and north to include Quemado. Mr. Duncan is one of our new lay missionaries, serving Grants and outlying points.

Mr. Young is at Lindrith and serving all of northwest New Mexico as far away as Aztec and outlying points along the Colorado line. His field is well organized into the Larger Parish Program. Mr. Wright is serving the Chama Parish, reaching a number of outlying points including the El Rito Normal School.

Mr. Reiter is serving the Pecos field and through the

140

north end of Estancha Valley including Pintada. Mr. Whittles, a new missionary, is serving the Claunch Parish, reaching Williard and many outlying points.

Roger Sherman is the Sunday School missionary serving Pecos Valley, fostering a number of mission Sunday Schools and carrying on an extensive program of visitation among isolated homes, often conducting services in homes where there is no other place. And Mr. Woods is the tenth man. He is pastor of our new church at Hobbs and receives his salary through the synod budget and the local support of the church. I am the eleventh, serving wherever I am needed as best I can. . . .

This summer we conducted about a hundred vacation Bible Schools, and conducted six young peoples' conferences besides the Sandia Conference. We organized some twenty new Sunday Schools, conducted about fifty teacher training courses, some twenty-five evangelistic meetings, held a number of Sunday School institutes, and were busy in many other ways.

Traveling Seminars

1940

IN MEETING PEOPLE in the East and across the country, I found that a lot of them had a desire to have a sure-enough, camping-out experience, to sleep in the open under the stars, eat around a campfire, and get off the beaten path. They wanted to see some of the real pioneering mission work in our country, to see the Spanish and Indian mission stations, to meet the missionaries, to see Grand Canyon and other outstanding points of interest.

So I suggested the camp type of traveling seminar. Bill Orr and I talked it over. I told Bill if he would take the guests to the mission stations, get missionary drivers and their cars, I would run the camp end of it. We got the necessary approval and decided to give it a try.

Bill got from twelve to eighteen cars each year, each driven by a missionary and led the caravan. I had to have about a hundred bedrolls — the old-fashioned cowboy kind, no sleeping bags or air mattresses. I bought the canvas in five-hundred-yard rolls, seven feet wide, and cut it into tarps eighteen feet long. Our son Jim and I made frames for outdoor toilets out of half-inch pipe, so we could take them apart for easy transporting. We had canvas hoods with zip-

142

pers, portable cook and work tables, a 500-gallon water tank, and all the kitchen equipment.

The bedrolls were all alike, so I painted a number on each one: when we reached camp, we would unload them in a big pile and tell the people to find their bedrolls by the number each had been assigned.

Each year Jim would get a big semitrailer truck from the oil fields, thirty-three to thirty-five feet long. A hundred bedrolls make a big pile and weigh about fifty pounds apiece. Each guest would have two or three suitcases, so we had a couple hundred bags.

I took a two-ton truck for water and supplies of all kinds, and we had a pickup truck for the chuck wagon with dishes, pots, and kettles, along with the large dutch ovens.

I never put up tents; the waterproof tarps on the bedrolls kept them dry.

I would feed the campers breakfast, then they would leave in cars with Bill Orr. They would meet me at noon for their lunch, at a place already agreed upon, after they had visited various mission stations. In the afternoons they would tour some more, and our crew would hurry to the next camping place to fix supper.

We traveled about two hundred miles a day, some 2,000 miles in all. It kept us busy gathering the wood, getting water and such, driving over backroads, and cooking three meals each day.

The first trip was a guess, as far as we were concerned, for we did not know how people would react to camp life. Many of them maybe sixty years old or older, had never even had a cup of coffee around a campfire.

On that first seminar we took the people off the train at Raton at 6:30 A.M. and gave them their breakfast. When night came we were all set in a rugged canyon with high cliffs on either side. We had one lady whose mother had felt she should not go on such a rugged trip; she had written and asked me to write and tell her daughter she couldn't come, to tell her the trip was too rough for her. I wrote back that it was going to be very rugged, but I didn't forbid her to come. The mother sent a blank check and said if her daughter was unhappy, to get her to the nearest airplane and send her home. She said the daughter had been served by a personal maid all her life and surely couldn't sleep on the ground.

Well, I didn't get the lady in question located until we called the roll around the campfire that first night. When her name was called, she jumped up and said, "I'm glad I am here." I think she would weigh about 150 pounds and she looked hearty; so I said to myself, "I'm not going to worry about her."

When we were ready to go to bed, thunder and lightning began to bounce around the big cliff above us. I asked the drivers to help people locate a bed ground and show them how to fix tarps for rain.

I thought all were bedded down when I heard someone — not crying, but bawling and wailing — down where the bedroll pile was. It was a woman and she kept saying "Oh, why did I ever get into a mess like this? Why did I come?" I knew it was this lady I've been describing, and that if I went there she would insist on me taking her to an airport somewhere. I sent our son, Ralph, who was eighteen years old, down to see her. He would let her weep on his shoulder. I told him to bed her down and tuck her in. I think he really did just that. Anyway, the next morning she came to camp singing, the happiest lark you ever saw. She adapted readily to living out in the open and was one of the best sports we ever had in camp.

In fact, I was surprised how quickly everyone adjusted to camp life. We never had any accidents, nor was anyone seriously ill. The seminar was self-supporting; we charged each guest only enough to pay his expenses.

I took the traveling seminar, which began in 1940, until the time of my retirement. We went every other year; I think it was the best and cheapest promotion the Board had, as everyone went back enthusiastic, and each made many addresses for the Board.

Dr. Merlyn A. Chappel, the head of the Department of Promotion for the Board of National Missions in New York City, was a key man in each seminar operation. He promoted it, handled all the paperwork, enrolled the guests, and planned the programs around the campfire each evening, with nearby missionaries speaking of their work to the guests. He made every trip with us and was a great inspiration to all of us. I cannot say too much about his great leadership; we never could have done it without him.

I doubt if there were three other men in the whole church who would have been crazy enough to take fifty to a hundred people on a 2,000 mile camping trip for twelve days, camping where maybe no one else had ever camped.

Young People's Camp Conferences

1927

IN THE EARLY DAYS of my ministry there were two
dreams that I had, two things that I most earnestly
prayed for. One of them was a dream for the young people scattered all over the ranch country and in the mining
camps and in the lumber camps and out on the homesteads.
Two or three could be found here and maybe ten miles
farther over the hills or across the plains you would find
two or three wonderfully fine people but never, never having the opportunity to get together in groups. "Someday," I
said, "I'm going to have a hundred of them together for a
few days when they can learn to play together, to sing together, and to worship together."

So one day we sent out about seventy cards and asked
the young people over a large area to meet us at Storm
Mountain on a certain date; they were to bring their bedrolls, dishes, and eating utensils, and we would furnish
everything else. We said if they could, to bring two dollars
to help pay the expenses, but if they couldn't to bring some
beans or potatoes or something from the home pantry — but
anyway, come. I thought maybe ten or twenty-five at best
might show up, but I think the whole group came.

146

At first, they were the most lost group of people you ever saw. A group would come in, see the other group and say "Hi," but they just didn't know how to get together, to play together. It wasn't until the first meal was served and as they went down the chuck line they began to talk and visit. They continued as they washed their dishes together in the big tubs of hot water that had been provided. Then we set up the little Billhorn folding organ, out on the edge of the mountain, and they gathered around for the first vesper service.

As we sat there on the side of this high mountain, you could look out yonder for a hundred miles or more across the great range country and see there nestled their homes and their families. It was one of those evenings with a glorious sunset, and we sat for a little while in perfect silence. It almost seemed irreverent to speak. And then the missionary's voice, "Be still, and know that I am God." The only sound we could hear was the wind rustling among the cliffs above us and down through the pine trees. It seemed as if it were the whispering of God's voice.

Later we sang together, and had the Scripture reading. We told once more the old, old story that never grows old. Then we moved a little farther over and built a campfire and they got out their guitars and sang songs of the open range and played games. In a little while we broke up to go to our bedrolls for the night, some of them sleeping under tents but most of them just sleeping out under the stars.

Well, we spent five days there together. Each hour, each day, I could see a whole new world and a whole new life opening up before these young people. Never could I forget that closing vesper service when we stood there and I talked with them a little bit, as we had been doing all week — about what it meant to be Christian people and how Jesus gave His life for them, and whether or not they would like to accept Him as their Savior and their Lord. Several of the older ones of the group that night made professions of faith

147

in the Lord Jesus Christ as their Savior. The next morning they were reluctant to leave, and as always there was the question, "Can't we come back? Won't we come back next year?"

And I said, "Yes, of course. We'll come back next year."

Then it was that we decided this had been such a wonderful experience that we coveted it for every young man and woman, every boy and girl, in all the range country. We were able to get more and better equipment, and we started out to take these young people's camp conferences to all of the areas in this vast range country. For some fifteen years we traveled with these trucks and this equipment, a great deal like a circus crew — having a camp here, closing at noon after five or six days, then tearing down the tents and loading all the equipment and driving through the later afternoon and often into the wee hours of the night, heading two hundred miles and more over the mountain roads and trails to another site where another group of young people would be waiting for us.

It was a job setting up the tents and getting ready for the first meal and the first part of the program. I've sometimes said I hoped there wouldn't be tents in heaven because we put them up and we tore them down until it seemed there wouldn't be anything left of them — or us.

We traveled literally from the Mexican border almost to the Canadian border — across New Mexico, Arizona, Colorado, Wyoming and South Dakota — having as many as twelve different young people's camps in one summer and sleeping every night for more than a hundred nights on the ground in our bedrolls. It became quite a task.

More than 17,000 young people have turned aside to be with us for a week in these camp conferences, and I have seen marvelous things happen in their hearts and lives. Wherever I go across this western country I can hardly stop in a village or a town, or preach in a church, but some of the young people, or people who were once young, will

148

come up and greet me and then talk immediately about the young people's conferences and the young people's camps.

Sometimes we used to wonder whether it was all worthwhile. We cooked every meal that was ever served to these 17,000 young people. We baked all the biscuits and cooked the beans and the beef and the stew and the steak, and I think I've cooked a billion pancakes because they had such hearty appetites.

A few years ago I had the privilege of preaching in one of our fine churches in the northern Rockies. It was in a beautiful sanctuary with soft light, stained glass windows, the lovely pipe organ and the robed choir back of me. At the close of the service as the benediction was pronounced, the choir started to march out. One of the young women broke ranks, came rushing up and looked up into my face and said, "I'll bet you couldn't guess in a hundred years who I am."

I looked down into those big brown eyes and said, "No, but I imagine you were in one of our young people's conferences somewhere back down across the range."

She said, "Yes, I was. I'm Janet."

"Oh, no," I said. "You're not Janet. You couldn't be Janet."

"Yes, I am Janet. Isn't it wonderful? I got my degree in seminary last spring and now I'm the director of religious education here in this church."

And then she looked up and the tears rolled down her cheeks as she said, "Thank you for coming that first time to our ranch. Thank you for letting me attend the young people's conference. I tremble sometimes when I think where I might be and what my life might be had you never come, and had I never gone to the young people's camp."

Then I thought of Janet the first time I had seen her. When I drove up to their ranch I found her helping her father with some calves out in the holding pen, branding

149

them. He roped a big calf, drug him up to the campfire, and yelled to Janet to hold him down. Janet pounced on him; he was just too much for her, but she did a good job.

Now I've heard the cowboys and the oil field workers and the lumberjacks try to express themselves in their moments of stress and great provocation, but I never heard anything like the language Janet used that morning for that calf. It was a language all her own.

I rode with her that afternoon as we were moving some cattle across the range, and told her about the young people's camp we were going to have farther over the other side of the mountain.

I said, "Wouldn't you like to come?"

"Well," she said, "what do you go up there for? What do you do?"

"We play games and we play baseball," I said. "We climb mountains. We sing together and have a Bible study." I guess maybe I put a little more emphasis on the mountain climbing and the baseball game than I did on Bible study.

"Well," she said, "Maybe I'll come and maybe I won't."

Janet came. And believe me she hadn't been in camp ten minutes until everybody knew Janet was there. It was just before the evening mealtime and I heard an awful commotion down in the brush. I rushed down; there was Janet with someone choking her, while she was kicking at another. She said, "I can lick any dozen of the so-and-sos, send them on."

I had wondered what would ever happen to Janet. Now here she was — this beautiful young woman with her Christian life and her Christian character. Something marvelous happened to Janet in those young people's conferences. And I had to bow my head and say, as I do over and over again, "Thank you, dear God, for the great privilege of baking pancakes, putting up tents, and having a part in the work of the building of Thy Kingdom."

150

Telling the Story
1957

FOR MORE THAN THIRTY YEARS I have been asked by the Board of National Missions to make at least one trip each year to tell the story of national missions to churches across the country. Each trip lasts from three weeks up to two months. Many years I have made two trips, one to the Atlantic Coast and one to the West Coast, speaking mostly on the work of Sunday School missions. Several times I addressed the General Assembly, and often have spoken to synods and presbyteries across the country in their regular meetings. There have been appearances before large groups of men, presbyterials and synodicals, high schools and colleges, and to many service clubs. And I have spoken many times to the Board of National Missions in their annual meetings.

I used to say to Mrs. Hall that a fellow needed a tongue of whang leather and a jaw of brass, as I often spoke four and five times a day. And this was for every day of the week except on Saturdays.

Several times I took Roger Sherman with me. When he was along we usually had the meeting in the fellowship hall where there was a stage or a high platform — or if in the sanctuary, we removed the pulpit furniture. We would take along our usual camp equipment — bedrolls, coffee pot, dutch oven, canteen of water, frying pan, and a box of wood. We would build an artificial fire with a strong light bulb and red paper, put a hot plate down in the fire, and really boil coffee and fry bacon. We would turn out all the lights in the auditorium, and light our fire by turning on the light in the campfire. Then we'd sit down on our bedrolls and tell to each other the stories of our missionary work, just as we have done so often in New Mexico, as if there was no one within miles of us. The setting made a very effective way of telling our stories.

On these trips I have spoken in every state in the Union including Alaska, except South Carolina, Alabama and Louisiana. I have had a gracious reception wherever I have spoken and met many wonderful people and made many friends. I always came home from these trips with a greater appreciation for my church with its burning heart and its zeal for the building of God's Kingdom on earth.

Hammers and Nails for the Kingdom

THE REVEREND WILLIAM M. ORR and I were received in the Rio Grande Presbytery at the same time. He came into the presbytery in order that he might accept the call of the First Presbyterian Church in Las Cruces. He was made chairman of the Committee of National Missions and with his great vision and concern for the people without Gospel privileges he became a tower of strength and help to the Sunday School missionaries. His wise counsel and guidance were a great help and inspiration to us.

He was out of the synod for several years but came back to us as our synod executive — in 1935, I believe it was — in which capacity he served until the time of his retirement. What a joy it was to work in good fellowship with him. Together we pioneered in many national missions projects. We traveled many new trails together and left the ashes of many campfires in strange places.

Since coming into the synod I have seen thirty-four new churches organized; twenty-four of them grew out of Sunday Schools started by the Sunday School missionaries. The

153

Sunday School missionaries built twelve new chapels and churches, and with the help of the volunteer labor from the communities, five new manses as well.

The missionary was the architect, construction foreman and laborer. How many hours of backbreaking work with shovel, axe, hammer and saw, the missionary put in will never be known.

Besides the churches and manses built in New Mexico, we were asked to help out in Arizona and Colorado. We built the church at Towaoc, Colorado on the Ute Reservation, the church and the manse at Payson, Arizona, and the church and manse at Kayenta on the Navajo Indian Reservation. These were not easy jobs; they were all in isolated places, far away from the source of supplies.

Kayenta, for instance, was the farthest post office from a railroad of anyplace in the United States. We hauled the material from Flagstaff, 170 miles away with old, worn-out trucks. I took five missionaries and our tools and camp outfits, and went over and set up camp in a pile of sand — the loose, blowing kind. This was in March when the sandstorms blow. In just thirty working days from the time we set up camp, we came away with the manse completed — with basement, bathroom and all the plumbing installed, and all painted inside and out.

One of the big jobs was the building of the chimney for the stove. It was too far to haul bricks from Flagstaff and too expensive, so we built forms and made bricks out of concrete. They are still standing.

We had a small two-hundred watt light plant and put in many hours of work at night.

I remember one night when we had an awful sandstorm. We were sleeping in our bedrolls and were literally buried in sand and had to dig ourselves out.

We had an electric cord running from the light plant, and hanging over the beds was a 100 watt light bulb. One of the missionaries couldn't sleep that night because every few minutes the light would flash from the static electricity coming in over the line in the wind and sand. He was convinced that the spooks were after us. Anyway, it was fun.

Other building projects we have shared in were the development of the Sandia Conference Grounds, the erection of the large tabernacles and kitchens and eating sheds at the camp meeting sites of the Nogal Mesa and the Mantosa Cowboy Camp meeting groups, and the erection of the health center at Lindrith.

How the Sandia Conference Grounds Began
1927

ANOTHER PROJECT Bill Orr and I pioneered in was the development of the Sandia Conference Grounds. For three years, beginning in 1924, the young people's conference for that area had met in Santa Fe. It was decided that for 1927 we would go out in the mountains. A site was secured from Dr. Cooper, who was pastor of the Presbyterian Church in Albuquerque and who owned the old Ellis Ranch in the Sandia Mountains. (He later offered to sell us a plot of ground with a beautiful spring and a stream of running water coming across it; I was able to get the money from the Nelson Dayton family in Minneapolis — $1,500 — to pay for it.)

As no car could drive into the conference grounds, the first job, with Bill as foreman, was to build a road. We didn't have an engineer nor any levels and that sort of thing, so the missionaries were called in, together with some of the other ministers of synod. We went up with our picks, shovels, and kegs of dynamite and started to blast out a road, over the hills and the mountain, up to the conference site.

It was not an easy task for soft hands and soft muscles. The hours were long but we came to enjoy it because we had visions of a road — not a great highway, but a road and a trail over which hundreds of people would travel to this dedicated and beautiful spot.

We would build a piece of road and I would charge over it in my old 1924 Chevrolet. If I could pull it, we would say, "That's a good road," and we would move on to another stretch.

When the road was completed, there was the job of erecting dormitories for men and women to sleep, a dining room where all could eat, a tabernacle where we could have our meetings, and a few rooms where families could have quarters. Most of us lived those first years in tents, and what a fine time we had.

For eleven years the synod, the synodical, and the young people's conference met at Sandia. How foolish perhaps we would sound today if we were to suggest that we have the three meetings at one time and in one place for three separate programs. But how wonderful it was back in those days when the minister could bring his own family and young people as we all gathered on the Sandia Mountain. The synod met in the tabernacle; the ladies met in the smaller chapel that had been built for them; and the young people for the most part held their classes out under the trees. A few sheds were built for classrooms to be used in case of rain.

Practically all the work had been done by ministers and missionaries. We developed the grounds so that we could sleep up to two hundred people and feed them in the dining room.

What a treat it was for the young people and the old people and all others to sit down together at the tables. We joined together in our devotional services, with the exception of the young people's vespers. It gave the young people a chance to know their missionaries who were all with their families. It gave them an opportunity to hear great, out-

157

standing ministers of the church, for each year we would bring in from some of the great churches the outstanding ministers of America. Our meetings lasted a week, giving us lots of time for the serious matters and the fun that are both so important.

Sandia Conference Grounds met a great need. As long as they live many of our young people all over the western country will remember as a high and holy and a sacred spot the Sandia Conference Grounds, and their wonderful hours and days spent there in good fellowship, and the inspiration that came to them for lives of Christian service.

Camp Meetings for Cowboys and Ranch Families

I SPOKE EARLIER of two enduring dreams for my ministry. One was for the young people, and the other was for the cowboys and the ranch families. Many of them, living way out fifty or a hundred miles from a church building or places of regular worship, never have the opportunity of getting together with other ranch people to enjoy the blessings of Christian fellowship.

By 1939 the synods and presbyteries were beginning to take over the young people's camps and conferences and provide for young people, so we had a little more time. At the close of our summer conference program in 1939 Roger and I vowed that the next summer, we would try to do something for the cowboys like we had been doing for the boys and girls. We would invite a large group of them to come and camp with us somewhere in the mountains; there we would have services of worship and we would sing and pray together.

It wasn't very long until we learned that others were having the same thoughts, others who felt the great need and desire to take the camp meetings to the cowboys. Dr.

Everett King, who had just come to the Board of National Missions as director of the Department of Sunday School Missions, went down to the old Boys Camp Meeting in Texas to be one of the ministers there that summer. Down there he met a great Christian layman, Joe Evans. Joe's people had helped to start the original camp meetings down there more than fifty years before, and for fifty years Joe had attended these camp meetings. He told Everett how he had a great urge in his heart to take the cowboy camp meetings to the ranch people of New Mexico.

Everett said, "Well, I have the men and we have the equipment, and if you'll throw in with us, somewhere next summer we will try a camp meeting in New Mexico."

So on the first of January, 1940, Everett King and I met with Joe Evans in El Paso. We went up to our room in the Hotel Del Norte, where we spent an entire day talking and thinking and planning about this great program of the camp meeting. We got down on our knees and in a season of prayer for guidance and help, we dedicated ourselves to this great cause.

A short time later, Roger Sherman and his brother, Forest, and I got in our car and with our bedrolls we drove through vast areas of the mountains in southeastern New Mexico seeking out a suitable campground. A little later Joe Evans came up; we gathered up a few of the local ranchers and spent two more days traveling in the canyons and to springs, looking for what we thought would be an ideal location for the camp meeting.

After we had looked at various places and the ranchers had said, "Well, we can use this." Or "That will be all right." But I could tell they were not satisfied. Finally Forest Sherman spoke something that had been on his mind: "I don't know just what you're looking for for this camp you are going to have, but I know a spot over yonder on Nogal Mesa. I don't know what there is about it, but somehow I can never ride up to that spot but I want to take off my hat."

160

All were immediately interested, and asked, "Where is it?"

"I guess about seventy miles across here," he said.

They looked at the sun and said, "We have time to make it. Let's go."

We got in our cars and drove up to Nogal Mesa. We parked and walked up to this great cliff where you could look out for two hundred miles in every direction. Unconciously, every man just lifted his hat. "This is it," they said. "This is the place."

But Forest said, "There's one thing I didn't tell you, and that is that there isn't any water on this mesa. I don't think you could dig a well deep enough to get water."

The others asked, "Where could we get water?"

"You could haul it from the pipeline over there," he said.

"How far?"

"Oh, I guess six or seven miles."

"Well," they said, "That's all right. We'll get water."

And then we began to talk and plan.

"Now we'll have all the preachers here we'll need," I said, "and we'll have just as many preaching services as you fellows think we ought to have." I wanted them to feel the responsibility and let them plan it as much as possible.

I thought that they'd say, "We ought to have two services a day; one in the morning and one in the evening. Instead, they said "We ought to get in four or five anyhow."

That sounded pretty heavy, but we agreed, and that is what we have always done — an early service about 8:45, another about 10:45, and another in the afternoon; then the prayer groups at 4:30 in the afternoon, men under the Prayer Tree, women in the tent; the evening service in the tent, and then a time of fellowship out around the campfire, the telling of stories and the singing of range songs and things of that nature.

As we continued to plan these fellows began to say, "I'll bring a beef." And another would say, "I'll bring a

161

beef." And then they talked about how they would feed the people. "We want to get the best cooks and we want the best food. We want to feed these people better than they've ever been fed."

Somebody said, "Old Santiago is the only man I know who could really cook for a group like this."

Somebody else asked, "Where is he?"

And the answer, "He's down on the old Cole Mean's outfit, I think, way down in the Davis Mountains."

One of the ranchers said, "If you think we ought to have Santiago, I'll get him."

When I raised the question of finances, how would we pay the expenses, they said, "Let's have it understood now, that there never will be anything for sale on these grounds. Nobody can buy a meal. Everything here is to be free."

Then one other spoke up: "Another thing, let's don't be passing the hat and taking collections and asking folks for money all the time."

They said, "We will have five hundred or six hundred people."

I said, "If you have that many people and you feed them three times a day, it's going to cost some money."

"That's in our department," they said, and so it was left that way.

We decided we would go up to the mesa the first of August, 1940, for our first camp meeting. We didn't print notices in the newspapers and announce it in the large churches across the range country. Mostly, it was just passed by word of lips from ranch to ranch and from range to range that some of us were going up there on top of Nogal Mesa on the first day of August, for a few days of camping together and for preaching services.

Roger and I went and set up the camp. Old Santiago came. Chairs were brought in and we were ready. We wondered how many folks would come, and thought if we had fifty people we would be pleased.

When we were singing our first hymn that night, I counted about 120 people in that first service. Before we went away five days later, we had about 500 there on the grounds.

How could I ever forget those first days?

The cowboys went out into the trees and picked out a beautiful old juniper tree for a cowboy prayer tree. We dedicated that tree just as any church in the synod is dedicated, as a place of prayer. The cowboys took branding irons, and they burned deep there on the trunk of the old tree the date of our first meeting — August 1, 1940.

I thought maybe when it came the hour of the men's prayer meeting, these fellows would think about the things they had to do and what business they had somewhere else, and would slip away.

To my amazement, every man and every boy on the ground went marching down toward the tree. They said everybody was welcome except the preacher. This was just for the men and so the preachers were not invited during those first meetings. But the cowboys went down, and in their own manner they conducted their prayer meeting. It was something like a testimony meeting as they just sat there and whittled and talked among themselves, each fellow saying something about his own life and his own problems, or about the camp meeting and how much it meant, what his hopes, his dreams, his plans were, not only for the camp meeting but for his family.

The closing service was something you don't forget. Gathered in that big tent, we hadn't put on any kind of a high pressure, emotional type of program. We just preached the Gospel of the Lord Jesus Christ, with all of His great love and claim for the hearts and lives of men. As we stood there we said, "It has been wonderful to be here. Tomorrow we are going back to the ranches and our homes. Maybe some of you would just like to come up here tonight and stand in front, and by that act say that you are accepting Christ as your Savior and you are going back down there

163

to that ranch as Christian families or as Christian people."

Well, they came, a great number of them. And we have seen marvelous things happen in their hearts and in their lives.

They said, "We must always come back. Every year we must come to this place."

"Yes," we said, "we will always come."

Then they said, "This is something we would like to take to all of the ranch people and the cowboys in this whole western range country. Can't you give your summers to it? Won't you try? Just start camp meetings all over the range country." And, they said, "If we can help, we will help." And they did. Some of these fellows have gone with me into Colorado, Wyoming and South Dakota to talk to other cattlemen and cowboys and ranchers about camp meetings in their locations.

And so we went back the next year and every year, and we had more and more people. It was just like a family reunion. How glad they were to see each other after some of them hadn't been together for a year, and then once more to sing and to worship and pray together.

We started a new camp meeting that next year over at Montosa, west of Magdalena. Here we had the same experiences, with the same results. We pushed out until today there are about a dozen of these camp meetings reaching out into Nevada and up to Wyoming and Montana and in the Black Hills of South Dakota; over in the sand hills of Nebraska, back down on the eastern and western slopes of Colorado, along with four of them in New Mexico and two in Arizona. I think about fifteen to twenty thousand different people every year turn aside from their ranches and their homes and go to one of these campsites and there live for those fine five days in wonderful worship fellowship.

I remember at one camp meeting, passing a group of women, as we were loading up the trucks and breaking camp. One of them said, "Come over here a minute." I did so, and she continued, "We have just been trying to say

164

among ourselves how much the camp meetings have meant to us and to our families and our communities, how wonderful it has been!" She paused, and said, "I was just saying to these ladies that I imagine that Heaven will be something like it has been here on the camp meeting grounds in this wonderful fellowship. Don't you think so?"

And I said, "Yes, I imagine it will be something like this."

We have tried to get the outstanding Protestant ministers in America to come each summer and preach for the cowboys. We have had some of the greatest ministers from our church and from the Methodist, Baptist, Christian and Episcopal churches. When we go to camp meetings we don't go just as Presbyterians and Methodists and Baptists, but we go there as Christian people. When the cowboys make their professions of faith, we urge them when they go back to the ranch to go to the nearest church and become members and become active Christians.

I have had many privileges in my work as a missionary and in ecclesiastical relations, but I think the greatest privilege that has ever come to me has been the privilege of being for many years the manager of the Ranchmen's Camp Meeting out here in this western range land.

Maybe a few words should be said about what it means to be manager of these camp meetings. Well, it means keeping in touch with the local committees of each camp meeting, to see that they have preparations made for the annual meeting — such as having wood, water, groceries, and the tabernacle or tent site cleaned. It means remembering such things as:

Securing two outstanding ministers to preach in each camp meeting, and getting a song leader. Ringing the bell just before each service to call the people on the grounds to worship. Leading the worship at the opening of each service four times a day. (You try to create the spirit of worship, the proper atmosphere for the minister to deliver his sermon. Doing it four times each day of the camp meeting, you have to be careful that you do not become professional.) Presiding at all business meetings. Seeing that the cooks have each meal ready to serve at the proper time. (In the eighteen years, I have never served a meal nor opened a service of worship five minutes late.)

Being responsible for all the equipment. Storing it for winter. Taking it out just before the start of a camp meeting tour. Greasing the trucks and seeing that they are operating properly. Loading the trucks with hymnbooks, a hundred iron folding chairs used for outdoor groups, a few bed tents, the large assembly tent that weighs 1,680 pounds, extra bedrolls all made up with fresh linen, and various other things such as the large bell. Then there's the chuck wagon truck that carries all the kitchen equipment — a large steel grill for cooking over the open fire, enough large 20-gallon pots, kettles and dutch ovens to cook for a thousand people, enough tin plates and cups, with knives and forks and spoons, to feed a thousand people at once.

When you arrive on the grounds you must put up the tents and other equipment. You drive the big truck about 7,000 miles before you finish the tour, and return home to unload and store all equipment for the winter. Quite a job — but more important, a wonderful opportunity.

Although I have been pushed aside by old Father Time and retired, the camp meeting still goes on. Tom Myers has taken over the responsibility and the leadership as manager of the camp meeting, and what a wonderful job he is doing! So I once more look back along the trail and see a dream come true and a prayer answered.

It has pleased me very much that some of the younger people, who made professions of faith in our little mission churches and came to know Christ through the conferences and other Sunday School missionary programs, have given their lives to the ministry. Some have come back to New Mexico, such as Wilber and Mona Randall, and Earl and Lois Harvey. Then there are the young men who came out from the seminaries and worked with us through the summer, then come back and give their lives, as Bill Lytle did for so many years, and Bill Muldrow. So to each one of them I say "Thank you."

I wish it were possible to mention the names of all of my fellow Sunday School missionaries; it has been my privilege to work with them. For me it has been a very rich and blessed fellowship. I am writing as just one of this group. I am sure each one could write the same thrilling stories. It has been a very rewarding experience to have worked with each one.

Family
1966

IN THE FALL OF 1915 something very wonderful happened for me. I met a very beautiful and charming young lady, Miss Lillie Bess Owens. I had gone to Roswell, New Mexico to attend a meeting of the synod. She attended several meetings of the synod and through a mutual friend we met. From then on for a while I had more business in Roswell than ever before.

The El Paso Presbytery asked me to come to its 1916 annual spring meeting in Barstow, Texas, prepared for examination for ordination. I had learned that Lillie Bess had an aunt living very near Barstow and asked her to ride down with me in my almost new Model T Ford car. It was about a two hundred mile drive. She accepted, and we had a wonderful trip in spite of the seventeen flat tires, caused mostly by mesquite thorns. (It was just a sandy road in those days; the thorns blew into the ruts, and the thin tires picked them up.)

I was a little more nervous during the ordination service, having Lille Bess sitting down there almost on the front row. On the way home I proposed to her and she said yes.

We were married on January 19, 1917 in her parents'

home in Weatherford, Texas. Our first home was in Lincoln, New Mexico, where she made me take my saddle off the footboard of the bed. She made a very wonderful adjustment from the fashionable school in Boston to the plain, western home of a cowboy missionary. Her love, loyalty and help made me a better man than I ever could have been without her.

Our three children have been a constant source of joy and satisfaction to us. I am afraid I cannot take much credit for their being the wonderful people they are, as Lillie Bess stayed home and raised them. To her goes the credit for their training.

I was away from home most of the time and we put lots of responsibility on the children at an early age. I could send them anywhere with a car or the trucks — to take messages or missionaries anywhere in New Mexico or Arizona. When we were conducting the young people's conferences and camps I often had to send them long distances over the mountain roads to gather up people or go after supplies. They often ran into difficulties — flat tires, truck breakdowns, rain, mud, or snow — but somehow we knew they would always make it in, and they did.

At one time the Board of National Missions operated a hospital and mission at Red Rock on the Indian (Navajo) Reservation, some thirty-five miles on west of Shiprock, New Mexico. At that time the roads were not marked or kept up and there was no regular highway from Albuquerque to Farmington across the reservation.

I was out with a camp and could not leave when word came of a bad siege of severe flu; the hospital sent word they had to have help. The only person I knew that we could get was a practical nurse in Pintada, a little mission point north of Encino, New Mexico. Jim was fourteen years old. I asked him if he could take the Model A Ford, bedrolls, chuck box, and such, and make the round trip of some six hundred miles to get the lady and take her to Red Rock.

He said, "Sure." I drew a rough sketch of the roads and

169

trails, pinpointed some landmarks, and told him to pull out. He made it and camped alone on the way home.

On another occasion when we had about a hundred young people in camp in the Black Range Mountains of southern New Mexico, I was called away for three days. I was doing the cooking for them over an open fire with the help of Ralph and Betty. I asked the two of them if they could run the camp while I was gone, do the cooking, and take care of everything. They did.

During World War II Ralph was in the South Pacific, and Jim was in Alaska. Betty and I were left alone with the conference program. She drove the truck all summer.

We felt the children could do everything. From the time they could toddle, they helped me in the camp program, teaching classes, conducting vesper services, or anything that needed to be done.

Jim's a minister, has three sons, and is now director of Ghost Ranch, a study center (more than 20,000 acres) owned and operated by the Board of Christian Education of our church.

Ralph for a number of years has been in the public school system at Farmington, New Mexico. He is principal of elementary schools, is an elder in the church, and teaches a Sunday School class. He has a wonderful family, four daughters, and one son.

Betty, now Mrs. Earle Bergquist, lives in Abilene, Texas. Her husband is an elder in the church and superintendent of the Sunday School. They have two daughters and spend more time at church than anywhere else.

God has blessed us with good health, and kept us from serious accidents. Of course we have had our anxious days and moments. I recall only one time in all the years when I was called home. When Jim was about eight years old, he had a long siege in the hospital. Lillie Bess called me from Clovis where I was preaching for a week, to come home and be with her. She could usually take care of the situations. I know she spent many sleepless nights in anxiety, but she was equal to all emergencies. I am sure I would have called for help many more times than she did.

I have driven more than two million miles in my car over all kinds of roads, day and night. I have been fortunate; in all those miles I have had only one small accident. I was going up a long, icy hill with a slow curve when I saw a pickup truck coming down, out of control. I pulled as far off the road as possible and stopped, thinking he could either stop or have plenty of room to go between me and the steep bank on the other side. By the time he got to me he was going almost sideways down the hill. I still thought he was going to miss me, but the rear end of his truck hit the right front fender of my car, tearing off the front fender. Even so, I was able to drive on to Denver, five hundred miles up the highway.

On one occasion Jim, Ralph, and I were to go to an isolated campsite in the Graham Mountains in Arizona, for a youth conference. Jim got sick and developed a high temperature so that we were quite concerned about him. I hated to leave, but felt I had to go on because the young people would be there expecting me. I left with the old truck heavily loaded. Ralph and Jim were to come in the car if Jim could make it, or Ralph would come on alone.

I drove up the winding road for miles, to the very top of the mountain. All the way, I was anxious and concerned about Jim and the family. In camp alone, with no one in twenty miles of me, I said to myself, if only there were a phone available so I could talk to home. I cooked and ate supper, still lonesome, then decided to take a walk, along a dim trail that led off through the tall timber.

Hidden in some heavy brush by the trail I saw a box and wondered what was in it. I went over and lifted the lid; inside was a telephone. I wondered if it was connected

171

to anywhere. I turned the crank vigorously and to my surprise, an operator said, "Number, please."

I had no idea where she was but I gave my home number and said, "Collect call." In a moment Lillie Bess said, "Hello" in Albuquerque. I had stumbled onto a Forest Service telephone.

I have never been so glad to hear her voice. It was a great relief to hear her say Jim was all right and that in a day or so he and Ralph would be on their way.

Sometimes I almost envied my fellow ministers who were pastors, because they could be home nights with their families. Sometimes it was painfully difficult to make a decision as to where my responsibility lay, with family who needed me or the work on the field that also claimed my time.

Lillie Bess made it much easier, for she always said, "You go ahead and we'll manage." Never once did she say, "Stay with us, don't go." When our only daughter, Betty, was born, I was far away in New Jersey and did not see her until she was weeks old.

The one thing I really looked forward to at retirement was that I could be home more. It is a real joy and privilege just to be with Lillie Bess and stay home some. I have not stopped altogether, as the speedometer on the car tells. I got a new car last fall and I note that in fewer than ten months it reads 20,000 miles.

The E. Z. Ranch

IN 1916 MR. AND MRS. LEE S. EVANS and their two
daughters moved out of the ranch country in the Davis
Mountains of Texas and bought a ranch out west of
Albuquerque, at the foot of Mt. Taylor. It was in isolated
country, not fenced nor in any way improved. They had to
build a house and fence the large tract of land.

They shipped in cattle and stocked it, put up many
windmills, and bought more and more land until it was
one of the largest and finest ranches in the Southwest.

Over the years we became dear and close friends with
them. We exchanged work — I would go out and help in
the roundups, often with Roger Sherman along, and when
they heard I was going to preach in a little schoolhouse or
church they would come and help. Their very presence
was always a great inspiration. They were always interested
in all the projects we started and were much help. When
we started the Cowboy's Camp Meetings they were active
in promoting them, and they helped me get meetings started
in other states — Colorado, South Dakota, and Arizona.

I had asked Rev. Charles Poling, who was at that
time pastor of the First Presbyterian Church in Phoenix,
Arizona, to come and preach in several camp meetings. In

this way the Evanses, both Lee and Lou C., got to know the Polings and so there were four couples of us — Evans, Poling, Sherman, and Hall — who enjoyed doing things together.

We were all near the same age. One day Lee said of the four of us, "We're all getting older and soon will have to retire from active service. Find us a plot of ground somewhere in the mountains off the beaten path where we can't be fenced in — a place where we can build our homes and where we can hunt and fish together. You boys look for such a place."

Roger and I located one place in the Capitan Mountains we thought might suit us but we came to no decision after taking Lee and Lou C. to see it. One day some months later Lee called me on the phone: "Don't look any further for our place to retire. I have it right here on our own ranch. There are about a thousand acres of land in the very southwest part, west of Bear Canyon, that we can cut off and it will be ours. When can you come to see it? I'll get Charlie Poling."

We set a date for the next week and the four of us drove up to the site right at the foot of Mount Taylor. We were excited over the location and the beauty of the spot, which even had wild turkey around, and we all agreed this was the place.

We began making plans right there. Lee said, "I'll bring in a sawmill and have them cut the lumber right here on our own grounds to build our houses."

We would have room to run a few cattle and we began to talk about a brand for our herd. Roger suggested that we use E. Z. for a brand.

Someone asked, "Why E. Z.?"

He replied, "It came so easy."

So we agreed on that, too. Soon the sawmill was cutting the lumber for our houses.

I really never had a real vacation and the Board had been after me to take off for two months. So in the fall of

174

1950, we went up to the E. Z. and camped; I got some Indian workmen to help me and we started our little mountain home, thinking it would be ready for us when we retired. The Indian men worked until the outside was completed. At Thanksgiving time Jim brought up a bunch of men from his church in Hobbs — including a fine carpenter-cabinetmaker and an electrician. I already had the plumbing and had a lot of the other work done, so with Jim's crew we just about wound up the job.

By the time the house was finished we decided that we couldn't wait for full retirement to move. In December, 1950, we moved in, and how wonderful it was. We counted as many as a hundred wild turkeys in our front yard; and had lots of wild game all about. There was a beautiful little stream nearby; it had never been stocked, but we stocked it with 400 rainbow trout, most of them under ten inches. We greatly enjoyed that little home, tucked away in the mountains.

I never left Lillie Bess up there alone, because it was so isolated — twenty miles from the post office telephone, and seventy miles from a doctor. Anyplace I went in my regular work I had to go through Albuquerque, where we had a small apartment that we kept when we leased our home. I would leave Lillie Bess there when I had to be away.

In 1962 Lillie Bess had a heart failure. Her heart just got weak. She was in the hospital for about a month. The doctor didn't want us to go back to our mountain home because of the altitude — nearly 8000 feet elevation — and the isolation.

So we moved into Plaza del Monte in Santa Fe, a home built by our Board of Pensions for retired ministers and their families. Here Lillie Bess had no responsibility, living with a wonderful group of people; many of whom we had known for years. She improved in health and was able to go with me wherever I went. The five years we had together

in this delightful home were really the crowning years of our married life.

Soon after I retired, and before we moved from the E. Z., we were having a big cattle roundup at the ranch. We were getting up about 3:00 A.M., riding hard all day branding calves and shaping up the herd. One day after we had made a big drive and had lots of cattle gathered, we had a lot of cutting to do on the herd. I was riding a big rough horse that stopped on his front feet; every time he would stop on a dead run trying to head a steer, it would almost kill me. I never had such a pain in my midriff. I thought it was just a stomachache but when the time came to get off my horse, I could hardly make it.

Lee Evans came over and asked, "What's the matter?" I said, "Just a stomachache." He wouldn't let me go in the branding pen after the day's work was over and they made me ride in a car instead of riding my horse to the corral.

Well, that night was a long, miserable one. The next morning I told the foreman, Bill Smith, to go ahead, that I was not going to ride that day. The others left for the day's work, taking our Jeep along to cover the rough country in the roundup.

By 10:00 A.M. I was sure enough hurting, then all at once I was able to relax after having my knees drawn up under my chin. For the first time I decided I had an attack of appendicitis, and I knew the old appendix was ruptured.

There was a painter working at the ranch, and he had a ten-year-old car that would run on about three cylinders. He said he would take us to Albuquerque so off we went, twenty miles on a rough mountain road to Laguna where he picked up my good car and made the fifty miles to the hospital. It was a long trip.

I told the doctor that I had a ruptured appendix. He couldn't believe it. I had been riding three days and was sore over every inch of my body so that I could not feel

176

any more soreness over the appendix than that in any other place.

We had arrived at the hospital Friday about noon, and they operated Sunday night. Sure enough, it was a ruptured appendix. I got along fine and in fifteen days or so I was out of the hospital. That was the only time I ever spent a full day in bed in my life.

1971

O N SATURDAY, DECEMBER 3, 1966, my beloved
Lillie Bess passed away. She often had said that
when the Lord called her home I likely would be
away preaching some place, and that is the way it happened.

She had planned to go with me that weekend; I was to
preach in Hagerman, New Mexico on Sunday. We wanted
to leave early to visit some dear cowboy friends along the
way. When I got up and called her, she said, "I don't think
I had better go. I have a little tickling in my throat and I
feel like I might be taking a cold. You go ahead and give
my love to all the folks."

I was a little concerned, but she insisted that she was
feeling fine, just didn't want to take the chance of having a
cold develop on the trip.

Our friends here at Plaza del Monte said she seemed to
be feeling fine and was very sparkling and happy all day,
especially at the evening meal in the dining room here.
After supper that Saturday evening Lillie Bess came down
to our apartment, turned on the television, curled up in
my big, old reclining chair, and went to sleep — a sleep from
which she was never to awaken. No one missed her until
she failed to come for her breakfast Sunday. Miss Schaffer,
our next room neighbor, came to see if she was all right and

found that she had slipped away into her eternal home. It was 9:00 A.M. before the sad message reached me. I got in my car and drove the long, lonely two hundred miles home alone. By the time I reached the Plaza, our son Jim and his wife, Ruth, were there waiting for me and by 9:00 P.M. all my family were there. Jim said he had never seen a more relaxed and peaceful expression on her face than she had that morning when he saw her curled up in the old chair, the lights still on and the TV still going.

I moved into a single room, and what a lonely, empty room it was.

In 1969 I was married to a gracious and lovely widow of a Presbyterian minister. Her name was Mrs. Edna G. Roberts. She had been a widow for nearly twenty years. We are near the same age. She was living here at the Plaza when we moved here in 1962, and she and Lillie Bess were close friends.

Edna and I had a rich and full life in the short time we had together before illness took her away from me in February, 1971. She was a wonderful companion and she greatly enriched and blessed my life with her love and deep devotion. I thank God for those months together.

In January, 1971 she developed serious trouble with hardening of the arteries that affected her memory. She began having great difficulty remembering anything, which caused a state of confusion for her. In February it became necessary to place her in a nursing home. She has the very best of care, has made a wonderful adjustment, and seems to be happy and content. The doctors give us little hope that she will ever be able to return to me. So once again I walk a lonely road, but how sweet and precious are the treasured memories that brighten my days.

All three of our children are still a great joy and comfort, and now I have three great-granddaughters to add to the ten grandchildren.

179

My home is still at Plaza del Monte, where I hope to spend the remaining days of my life. The address there is Plaza del Monte, P. O. Box 1888, Santa Fe, New Mexico 87501.

Recognition by Synod

1957

ONE OF THE GREATEST SURPRISES of my life came to me while attending the annual meeting of the Synod of New Mexico. The printed docket was vague in announcing the program for Wednesday evening, saying only that it would be a program of national missions with Dr. J. Earl Jackman presiding. Dr. Jackman was the director of our Sunday School Missions Department; his office was with the Board of National Missions in New York City. It was a great privilege for the Synod to have him visit us.

Lillie Bess and I were sitting way back in the congregation when, after only a brief devotional service, Dr. Jackman asked Ralph Hall to come to the pulpit.

It turned out that several members of my family were there, but had kept out of sight all day. The grandchildren had a great time watching us but staying out of sight, hiding behind hedges and such places.

We were made to feel humble and grateful that the synod would take a whole evening out of its busy program to recognize us.

I am sorry I do not have copies of the various tapes that

were played, or of the gracious things that were said by so many who spoke in the program. I do have a copy of what was written for that evening of October 16, 1957:

-Synod Recognition For Ralph Hall-

Dr. Jackman:

For nearly half a century, Ralph, you have been a minister in the Presbyterian Church. The things you have done for Christ, and for all of us who have known you, can't ever be counted. You have been a preacher ... a missionary ... an organizer ... a planner, a leader, a dreamer. Your work has reached from the farthest outpost of the lonely West to the busiest offices of the church. Your achievements in dozens of fields have outnumbered all that any of us could hope to accomplish in even one of them.

Yet, your greatest good and your inmost love have always been where they — and you — are now: Out here among the ranch folk of the West, bringing them to God, and bringing the word and the love of God to them.

This was your life, Ralph. And now, as we bid you an official farewell, all of us here and many, many others who are here only in their thoughts, make this little presentation of our regard for you.

This, Ralph Hall, is *Your* Life.

You were born in 1891, Ralph, in your parents' home in the ranch country of Texas.

Your parents were ranchers, and the early years of your life were the years of a ranch boy. You lived in the sparsely populated plains of West Texas, and you didn't see much, in your boyhood, of churches or towns. But your parents were Christian parents, and the training you received was of a kind that could be a model for any Christian family today.

Something happened in those years that had a significant effect on your life. How could we better relive that than to hear it from your own voice on this tape recording?

(Tape, beginning, "you know, we lived way out
there" and ending . . . "I wanted to be a missionary.")

Well, there were ten children in your family, Ralph,
five of you boys and five girls. Nine of them are living now.
Some of them are here tonight to share this service of
recognition for you. We want to have a word from that
wonderful family now, from your youngest brother, George
Hall . . .

(George's remarks.)

The years passed swiftly, but the early purpose of your
life never varied, and found its fulfillment in your ministry
to the wide ranges from Midland to Seminole and from
Roswell to Post. You traveled on horseback, and with those
famed bronc horses, Geronimo and No Carrie, who traveled
as a team only when their tails were tied together.

It was in this period that the Presbyterian Church, seeing in you and your work a spark of rare value, asked you to
consider ordination as one of its ministers. After what you
have called the most soul-searching decision of your life,
you accepted this new challenge, and were ordained by the
Presbytery of El Paso. Resolved not only to carry on your
ministry, but to add to it by further study, you often made
the long ride to Roswell, to study with Dr. Charles Dowling.

And something besides study came into your life there.
She was a pretty girl from your own state, a graduate from
a school in faraway Boston and a teacher in Roswell. Her
name was Lillie Bess Owens, and soon a courtship began
and flourished with picnics to the White Mountains, among
the pines you both still love so well. You were married to
this wonderful girl on January 19, 1917.

There could not have been a better wife for a young
minister such as you were, and no better partner for the
years that lay ahead. When the way was difficult, she en-
couraged and helped you. When the increasing demands of

183

your calling took you away from her and your home, she released you to a service you were peculiarly fitted to fulfill.

Let us pause a minute here to call her up here to your side, where she has always been. Will you sit there beside your husband, Mrs. Hall?

In the years that followed, three children came to your home: Betty, your daughter, now Mrs. Earle Bergquist, of Abilene, Texas. (She comes on and greets them, without any comment from her.) And Jim, who needs no introduction to this synod, who is pastor of the First Presbyterian Church of Hobbs. (Jim likewise comes on without comment.)

And Ralph, principal of a public school in Farmington, New Mexico, who speaks for all of them in this further word about your family.

(Ralph's remarks.)

They were busy times, those early family years — although in reality your full life has known no other times. You held brief pastorates in Quanah, Post, and La Porte, Colorado. Here two things which were to loom large in your life had their beginning. You saw a need for a recreation building in La Porte, and under your own direction and with your own help in the labor of it, a large gymnasium was built to serve the community. In La Porte, too, your work of taking the word of God to the ranchers was expanded; and it was during your stay there that you were asked to become a Sunday School missionary by Dr. John Somerndike, who was to become your counselor and your great friend for many years.

Your commission read that you were to be a "missionary to the ranch people of the West"; and whatever other directions your trail led you, you always came back, as you do still, to this commitment.

You returned to New Mexico then, and in this state

184

again met a man who had, and has, been another special highlight in your life.

Your association with this man had started in an unusual way. It was before your ordination and before your marriage that you had ridden one day into the headquarters of the Sherman ranch near Seminole, Texas. Your reception was not the kind that would be welcomed by a young preacher.

But something in you, and in the thing you had to give them, made a change in the people there. One of them is here now — Roger Sherman, your long-time friend and fellow missionary — to tell about what grew out of that day:

(Roger, telling of giving Ralph a bad time, seeing him prove himself, and skipping on to relate how he was one of Ralph's early converts.)

There began, in New Mexico, your widespread ministry as a missionary to those who knew few, if any, other men of God. You followed the rough roads and the dim trails to their ends, and you nurtured the new homesteading communities, the sawmills, the mining camps, and the lonesome cowboys' wagon camps, in the spirit and the love of the Kingdom.

If any of us here can believe in the true communion of saints, Ralph, then we know without a doubt that men like Uncle John Henry, who rode with you on the King's Highway in those early years, are sharing in this fellowship with us tonight.

In this period, too, you began to be called to another service — that of telling the story of your work in the West to the churches, the boards and the agencies of the church in the East. These were not pleasure trips, these long eastern journeys. You were called on to be gone from your home for as much as three months at a time, and it was during one such trip — during your absence when you could not

185

be released to return — that your only daughter was born. But you accepted them cheerfully and unstintingly, and your arduous work here too, found a reward. For in this way, deeply and personally, the Presbyterian Church as a national organization learned of the vital importance and the unending significance of Sunday School missions. A man who once heard you in such a lecture, and treasures it as a great influence in his life, has a note to add here:

(The Reverend Charles Carson, executive in the Synod of Maryland: tape recording.)

Back home, wherever you were, things were happening. You saw the need for church buildings in the scattered communities and settlements of the West. There was none but you to do it — and so in many ways you did it yourself. Sometimes you were architect, contractor, foreman and laborer all at once — and always without any extra pay except your love for the job. Often you were cook as well, preparing meals for the men who worked for you on the church building jobs.

The ways were not just busy, but sometimes, painful. There was the day you fell from a truck loaded with lumber, and broke your arm. Yet, an hour later, your friends found you still trying to crank the truck so that you could get on with the work. Another project was a Towaoc on the Ute Indian reservation, where you worked with your helpers in bitter and cold sandstorms to provide a mission church with a place to meet.

And speaking of buildings, Ralph, it was during this time that another project came into being which was to mean much to you, and to gain much from you as well. There was no place for the young people's camps to be held in the Synod of New Mexico, and these conferences had to be staged at sites that really were inadequate and ill-suited to them. At last a new site became available — high

in the wilderness of the Sandia Mountains, with not even a road to reach it. But those high hills were not too high for you and the other devoted men who worked with you. With another of your countless friends, you staked a road into this isolated but beautiful area, and with him, and others, you built the buildings and laid the groundwork for a conference ground that was to become a high and holy place for many young men and young women through the years to come. The man who worked beside you in the building of the Sandia Conference Grounds is here now to shake hands with you once again: Bill Orr.

(No comments from Mr. Orr.)

And Bill Orr has been associated with you on another great venture, too — the unique traveling seminar of the Southwest. To tell more about that, though, listen to the voice of Dr. Merlyn Chappel:

(Tape recording.)

Some of the laymen who also shared in these seminars as members of your camp crew, are waiting now to say hello:

(They come on, shake hands.)

Your work at Sandia continued, along with the other aspects of your ministry, past the building of the camp. For some eleven years you were further called upon to maintain it — revamping it and preparing it to be opened in the chill of spring, and doing everything from draining water lines to storing the mattresses from its bunk beds in the fall. The work, and the planning, too — once again, these two full-time phases of a project were part of your life.

At Sandia, there were buildings and accommodations. But there were other young people in isolated sections far

187

away from this site, and in your life you dreamed of camps and conferences where they, too, could meet together and share the fellowship of each other and the Lord. So, another branch of your work for Christ's Church was founded: the establishing of young people's camps off the highways and in many states, but close to your heart and close to the cause you served. The youngsters came from hundreds of miles around, sometimes, in these back-country areas, and their tuition in those depression days might be a little money, a sack of beans, a chunk of beef — or nothing at all.

Along with the assortment of helpers you acquired along the trail, you were a little of everything in these hardy but heartening days. You were a conference leader, and a cook, and a planner and coordinator. If there was no other transportation, you drove your battered truck along the rocky roads to bring in the boys and girls. They slept under the stars and they lived in the rough, and they enjoyed a fellowship and a richness in Christ that could have come to them in no other way.

Oftentimes in these conference trips you were aided by — or saddled with — the help of young college students or fledging ministers who made up part of your staff. Of these there are many. Not all of them could possibly be here now to tell you how much those days meant to them. One who could be here is a young man who went on to become a minister, and now is retiring moderator of the Synod of New Mexico: Bill Lytle:

(Comments by him.)

And in more recent years another man was influenced by your life in choosing his place of service: Bill Muldrow.

(Comments by him.)

There was so much to do in the life of Ralph Hall, and so little time for the honors and commendations that grew out of it, the Doctor of Divinity degree which was bestowed on you by the Grove City College, Grove City, Pennsylvania, for instance. You were invited to go to that eastern college one year, to receive its honorary D.D. degree. You could not go; there was work for you at home in the West.

And so, because your work for your ministry left no time for you to be away, the honor instead was sent to you. Through Dr. Everett King, as its special representative, Grove City College bestowed on you the cap and robe, and the degree of Doctor of Divinity.

The bestowing of this degree came, then, not in the ivy halls of the college, but in the Big Tent of a camp meeting ground known as Nogal Mesa. And therein is another shining chapter in the story of your life.

It started, really, in the minds of three men: Joe Evans, Everett King, and you, Ralph. You first discussed it, the three of you, in a hotel room in El Paso. You planned on it, and you prayed about it, and out of that night's plans and prayers came the first Ranchmen's Camp Meeting at Nogal Mesa in 1940. It was a program that was to grow until thousands of ranch people, in camp meetings through six states, were joining in the services of worship, drawing close to God under the old Prayer Trees.

The first meeting place, there at Nogal Mesa, was chosen when your old friend Forest Sherman described it as "a sort of spot where I just have to take off my hat every time I ride by it." That was many years ago; now Nogal Mesa and the other eleven Cowboy Camp Meetings [in Nebraska, South Dakota, Wyoming, Nevada, Colorado, New Mexico (4), Arizona (2)] have come to be important and lasting phases of the Sunday School mission work.

Many a ranch family which has no other church finds peace and inspiration at the camp meetings each year. Possibly no other single phase of your ministry has become more widely known.

One of those original three men who planned the first

189

of these camp meetings sends you his greetings now. Here is the voice of your long-time pal, Joe Evans:

(Tape from Joe Evans.)

Through all these long years, Ralph — forty-five years as an ordained minister of the Presbyterian Church — you sought no personal glory and claimed no personal fame. But true honors and true fame can't help but come to such a man as you.

You have been the subject of many articles in magazines of national and significant stature and circulation — *The Christian Herald,* the *Saturday Evening Post, Time, Coronet, Presbyterian Life,* and others. Your many addresses before the General Assembly and your many other lectures have won you a place as one of the most widely heard and respected speakers in the Presbyterian Church. Your work in the boards and committees of that church has made you known wherever its creed is spread. There were movies, too — made by your church to show the rare value of your work. Let Dr. Fred Thorne, who helped to make them, say a word:

(Tape recording.)

Greater than all these honors, though, are the deep and abiding friends you have found along the way. Some of these you have already seen tonight. A few of the others are here, too, and come now to briefly say hello as this service nears its close.

(Rancher friends, all those here, to be brought backstage by Roger and come on now to shake hands. Convert at camp meeting, Marvin Ake, to say few words, is there.)

This is your life, Ralph Hall. The miles behind you have been long, and many of them hard. They have taken

190

you to the highest esteem of your church and your fellow Christians. And they have brought you back, at last, here to your beloved land of the West.

None of us can say all that is in our hearts for you. Let us say, for all here, and for the many others who are with you in their thoughts, all our wishes for God's best blessings to you and yours in the years ahead, and His continued blessings upon all the works that you have done in His name.

(Jackman to close with presenting of greetings from those unable to come, the purse, and a prayer of benediction.)

A Moment To Pause and Ponder

VERY SOON I WILL BE celebrating my eightieth birthday. For a moment I pause to look back along the long trail. How very wonderful it has been. There have been the dark days, the days of walking in the valley of shadows, but to these memory gives a soft and a mellow glow. Then there have been the mountaintop experiences, the times of walking through the green pastures, time to tarry beside the still waters. I have known the times of failures, of mistakes and defeat. For these I am truly sorry.

As I travel back along memory's road, I do not hear the applause or acclaim of the throngs of people. I do not see the great cathedrals of worshipping masses. What I do see are thousands of humble homes, at the ends of dim trails, the thrilling voices of welcome, the holy moments of worship at the family altar, little dimly lighted one-room schoolhouses filled with lonely people eager to hear the preaching of the Gospel. I see the many times of standing by a smoldering campfire, talking heart to heart to a group of cowboys about my Lord, the grip of a thousand hands that said more than could have been said by words. My heart is made tender by precious memories of the many altar places — back along the trail.

192

Now that my steps have grown more tottering, my eyes do not see so clearly, my hearing is not so keen, all remind me that out there not faraway is the end of the trail.

How glorious, lovely and beautiful is the twilight of life's evening time, when you have the Son of God, the Savior of men, who has followed you all the days of your life with grace and undying love, and you hear Him whisper once again, "Lo, I am with you always even to the end of the trail."

When you have gathered with me there at the end of the trail to pay your respects and tributes of love, come, I beg you, not with mournful songs of hopelessness and despair. Rather, pull out all the stops and press down on all the pedals of the organ. Let music of the great "Hallelujah Chorus" ring out with its songs of victory, triumph and praise.

I bear testimony that the yearning and the longing of that small lad's heart so many years ago, have been satisfied and fulfilled, that his dreams have come true, and his prayers have been answered.